Jewish Voices for Palestinian Rights

Eliza Tenison

Table of Contents

Abstract

- How does dominant rhetoric in support of Israel continue to negate Palestinian history and identity?

- What are the boundaries of legitimate political speech in American Jewish discourse regarding Israel? Who crosses them, and what are the consequences?

- What leads certain Jewish dissenters to cross intracommunal boundaries about Israel?

- How do these boundary formations shift according to context?

- What does reinventing Jewish identity in solidarity with Palestinian rights look like?

According to the corpus that I examine, not only are dissenters speaking out in support of Palestinian rights, but they are also asserting for themselves what it means to be Jewish. Such assertions of reinvented self-understanding challenge the dominant narrative of Jewish identity as unequivocally Zionist: "Israel, right or wrong" (Waxman, *Trouble* 55).

Through textual analysis, I show how this rhetoric of dissent redraws the contours of Jewish identity as a mode of ethical relations that heeds the call for Palestinian freedom. At the heart of this reinvention of identity, Jewish dissenters reframe Holocaust memory and the threat of antisemitism as interconnected with other forms of ethnic and racial prejudice, not uniquely separate from. Through this reframing, the call for justice from the Palestinian "Other" becomes audible.

As a method, rhetorical criticism is the analysis of the symbolism and their effects in discourse. In chapter one, I start by delineating a rhetorical genealogy of Zionism's erasure of Palestinian life and history. In chapter two, I continue to trace the rhetorical genealogy through the trope of the antisemitic Arab terrorist Other, an effect of what I refer to as Zionist rhetoric of

existential threat. Situated in genealogical context, the case studies of dissent show the

imperative for reinventing identity as a way toward justice.

Chapter three examines first-person identity reconstitution by critics Peter Beinart and

Sara Roy. First-person identity constitution analyzes how authors and speakers constitute their

identities in discourse through narrative about their personal realities, or what Dana Anderson

calls "expressible self-interpretation" (11). I show how a critical rhetoric of first-person narrative

can be a transformative cultural resource that reinvents identity as an ethical practice in relation

to otherness. I look to the work of Judith Butler for a philosophy of ethical relations.

Chapter four examines the rhetorical refusal of ethnonationalist birthright through the

lens of the universal audience. For rhetorical theories of the universal audience, I draw upon the

work of Chaim Perelman and Lucie Olbrechts-Tyteca, Janice Fernheimer, John Schilb, and

Antonio de Velasco. In chapter five, I turn toward in the practical application of audience-based

pedagogy in the writing classroom as a way to cultivate rhetorical awareness in students.

While Holocaust-centered Zionist rhetoric continues to claim that Jews in the Diaspora

need the State of Israel for Jewish security, Israel also frames its geopolitical position as

constantly under antisemitic existential threat and attack. Regardless, for many Jews, the State of

Israel represents a necessary place of safety and refuge.

In the artifacts that I examine, dissenters call into question the exclusionary

ethnonationalist notion of Jewish safety and reframe Jewish security as bound up with the

freedom and rights of all oppressed people. Jewish dissenters utilize first-person narrative,

rhetorical refusal, and dissociative techniques to break the links in dominant discourse that attach

the threat of antisemitism to the need for a hypermilitarized Jewish state.

As much as ethnonationalist discourse would like to dictate and cement a certain type of identity narrative as fixed and final, scholarship across the humanities and social sciences for decades has shown us that identity is no such thing. Identity is not a fixed entity but rather an iterative process that is always open to change. We see this fact when dissenters refuse the erasure of Palestinian life and history and work to integrate Palestinian perspectives in Jewish narratives of self-understanding about Israel.

Reinventing Jewish identity in solidarity with Palestinian rights means incorporating Palestinian narratives into Israel education, not as an empty gesture of inclusion but as a fundamental restructuring that understands Zionism from the perspective of Palestinian history and dispossession.

Chapter 1

Zionism's Third Persona

This dissertation is about the ways that American Jewish rhetoric of dissent redraws the contours of Jewish identity as a mode of ethical relations that heeds the call for Palestinian freedom. Dissenters enact a reinvention of Jewish identity through criticism of Zionism and illiberal Israeli policies toward Palestinians. Although there is an abundance of scholarship on what is widely referred to as the Israel-Palestine conflict in political science, international relations, history, Middle Eastern and North African studies, Israel studies, communication studies, and feminist, queer, and ethnic studies, there is a somewhat surprising lack of literature in rhetoric. Rhetoricians such as Matthew Abraham, Robert C. Rowland, and David A. Frank have begun to pave a foundation for Palestine and Israel in rhetorical studies. We need further research into the rhetorical nature of contemporary ethnonationalist ideology and the material conditions that undergird the circulation of its narratives. An overwhelming imbalance of power, such as monetary asymmetries, state violence, high-tech biopolitical surveillance, and propaganda infrastructure, upholds and legitimizes the Zionist policies of Palestinian erasure. While Rowland and Frank examine dominant narratives in the conflict and Abraham investigates academic controversies around the question of Palestine, my research shows that dissenting rhetoric can be a resource for cultural transformation and that the reinvention of identity must also be accounted for when reimagining a future of decolonization and cohabitation.

In Zionist framing (Jewish ethnonationalist ideology), Palestinians constitute an absent presence in public debate and cultural representations. I conceptualize this disavowal as Zionism's Third Persona. Third Persona is a rhetorical concept first articulated by Philip

Wander, which he defines as an ideological maneuver that constructs the identity of the intended audience through what it is not. Whereas First Persona is the "I" in discourse (the author or speaker and their intent) and Second Persona is the "you" (the target audience in a given rhetorical situation), the Third Persona is an audience perhaps implied but not directly addressed; a tertiary audience that is somehow alluded to in the message and thus constitutive of it yet disavowed nonetheless. The Second Persona, Wander writes, is the author's or speaker's target audience, the audience that "exists as a fact and an invitation. [...] What is negated through the Second Persona forms the silhouette of a Third Persona—the 'it' that is not present, that is objectified in a way that 'you' and 'I' are not" (209). Ideologically, Third Persona becomes a strategy of symbolic erasure through marginalization and dehumanizing stereotypes in discursive networks of knowledge-power.

Zionism's Third Persona is the dominant narrative frame from which Jewish rhetoric of dissent emerges and speaks back to. This is the underlying assumption and starting point of my rhetorical criticism. In the following chapters, I illustrate both how Zionism's Third Persona is integral to Zionism's logic of territorial expansionism and how dissenters challenge this logic by reinventing the relationship with Palestinian rights. As Zionism's Third Persona, Palestinian self-representation is disregarded and denied, and representations *about* Palestinians through the shared American and Israeli dominant frame tend to objectify them as: (a) antisemitic terrorists, (b) rejectionists to Israel's peace offers, (c) corrupt and unable to self-govern, and (d) self-inflicted victims.[1] Today, there are approximately five million Palestinians who live under Israeli military law with no citizenship status or rights.

---

[1] Other studies point to the same conclusion regarding the objectification and systematic exclusion of Palestinians. See Chomsky, *Fateful Triangle: The United States, Israel, and the Palestinians* and "Middle East Terrorism and the American Ideological System"; Elgindy, *Blind Spot: America and the Palestinians, from Balfour to Trump*; Judis, *Genesis: Truman, American Jews, and the Origins of the Arab/Israeli Conflict*; Karmi, *Married to*

Through a case study of representative texts,[2] I delineate a Jewish discourse of dissent that recuperates the Palestinians as partners of dialogue. As Palestinian self-representation remains marginalized as the Third Persona in dominant American perceptions of Israel's right to exist and defend itself, Jewish dissenters work to shift this view not only in terms of outward perception but also of self-understanding. Since 1948 and especially post-1967, being Zionist or "pro-Israel" has become bound up with what it means to be Jewish in the United States, and even part of what it means to be American for non-Jews.[3] According to the rhetoric of dissent that I examine, not only are dissenters speaking out in support of Palestinian rights but they are also asserting for themselves what it means to be Jewish.[4] Such assertions of reinvented self-understanding challenge the dominant narrative of Jewish identity as unequivocally Zionist: "Israel, right or wrong" (Waxman, *Trouble* 55). Dissenters reconstitute identity as an ethical relation to otherness with the potential to transcend ethnonational boundaries.

In this way, I am studying Jewish rhetoric of dissent as a rhetoric of identity. What rhetorical strategies of resistance do Jewish American dissenters utilize to reframe the dominant narrative about Israel, and hence what it means to be Jewish? I examine three main facets of this rhetorical situation that I formulate in terms of First, Second, and Third Personae. For the First Persona, I am interested in dissenters who speak out "as a Jew" or self-reflect on Jewishness with regard to Palestinian rights. This leads to the Second Persona: as a Jew in an appeal to other

---

Another Man: Israel's Dilemma in Palestine; Khalidi, *Brokers of Deceit: How the U.S. Has Undermined Peace in the Middle East*; and Said, *The Question of Palestine.*

[2] Textual artifacts that I examine are in the English language and based in a U.S. context.

[3] See Kaplan, *Our American Israel: The Story of an Entangled Alliance*; Magid, "The Holocaust and Jewish Identity in America: Memory, the Unique, and the Universal"; Silberstein, "American Jewry's Identification with Israel: Problems and Prospects"; Waxman, *Trouble in the Tribe: The American Jewish Conflict over Israel*; and Woocher, *Sacred Survival: The Civil Religion of American Jews*

[4] See also Omer, *Days of Awe: Reimagining Jewishness in Solidarity with Palestinians.*

Jews, particularly when the target audience is the mainstream U.S. Jewish community.[5] Thirdly,

I am interested in the ways that this appeal to a Jewish audience simultaneously functions as a

response to Palestinian suffering and calls for justice. Thus, I argue that the Jewish dissenter's

appeal to what rhetorician Janice W. Fernheimer conceptualizes as "the universal Jewish

audience" (49) also functions as act of solidarity with Palestinian freedom. The appeal here is

two-fold: American Jewish dissenters are both attempting to reinvent the universal Jewish

audience as a definitional concept of identity *and* establish an ethical relation of solidarity with

Palestinian rights. In fact, it is primarily through the ethical relation to Palestinian rights that the

universal Jewish audience is substantively redrawn.

For mainstream U.S. Jewish audiences, I am necessarily suggesting that the Jewish

subject position leverages a certain rhetorical privilege and command in criticism of Israel that

non-Jewish critics do not. In some ways, this is what rhetorician Dana Anderson calls the *"ethos

effects"* of the rhetoric of first-person identity constitution (100, *original emphasis*). However,

this is not to suggest that U.S. Middle East policy regarding Israel-Palestine is only of concern to

American Jewry, or that only Jews can legitimately speak about the State of Israel, least of whom

would also include Palestinians. Rather, I am interested in the rhetorical situation as such to

explore and specify the realms of tolerated dissent in American Jewish discourse regarding

---

[5] I use the phrases "mainstream U.S. Jewish community" and "American Jewish establishment" according to the context. While there are differences between the two, there remain key overlaps. The American Jewish establishment, broadly speaking, comprises recognized organizations such as The Jewish Federations of North America and those listed with the Conference of Presidents of Major American Jewish Organizations (Conference of Presidents). Conference of Presidents has over fifty member organizations, for example: American Israel Public Affairs Committee (AIPAC), the American Jewish Committee, American Friends of Likud, Americans for Peace Now, Hillel: The Foundation for Jewish Campus Life, Jewish Community Center Association, Zionist Organization of America, Jewish National Fund, and the Anti-Defamation League. The mainstream Jewish community refers to many Conference of Presidents organizations in addition to organized local communities such as synagogues and their affiliated members, youth groups, and religious schools. Fernheimer uses the phrase "'recognized Jewish community' as an umbrella term to include all mainstream Jews and the organizations affiliated with them" (48). Waxman uses the phrase "American Jewish community" to variously describe localized Jewish communities, the pro-Israel lobby in Washington, DC, and the American Jewish communal establishment (*Trouble* 3).

Israel. This dissertation shows that breaching the realm of tolerated dissent is not only a political offense, but also that dissenters locate and reveal the linchpin on which Zionist constructions of Jewish identity and history depends. The reinvention of identity appears so threatening because dissenters remove the linchpin and the Zionist rhetoric of justification collapses.

My main methodological goal includes a better understanding of prevailing accounts of Jewish-Palestinian antagonism and to generate knowledge of alternative relations. In order to show how dissenting rhetoric emerges from and speaks back to Zionism's Third Persona, I start by delineating a rhetorical genealogy of the concept with the beginning of Zionism. In chapter two, I continue to trace the rhetorical genealogy through the figure of the antisemitic Arab terrorist Other. Situated in genealogical context, the case studies of dissent show the imperative for reinventing identity as a way toward justice. This dissertation asks, how does dominant rhetoric in support of Israel continue to negate Palestinian history and identity? What are the boundaries of legitimate political speech in American Jewish discourse regarding Israel? Who crosses them, and what are the consequences? What leads certain Jewish dissenters to cross intracommunal discursive boundaries about Israel? How do these boundary formations shift according to context? What does reinventing Jewish identity in solidarity with Palestinian self-determination[6] look like?

---

[6] I distinguish between the individual human right of self-determination which entails the freedom to live one's life, and the idea of national self-determination which strives to or establishes collective sovereignty and statehood. The distinction and use of terms such as liberation, self-determination, and national independence in the Palestinian freedom movement is an ongoing debate. Palestinian scholar Ibrahim Abu-Lughod writes, "The Question of Palestine is largely one of self-determination. But whose self-determination and just what is self-determination anyhow?" (410).

In *The Question of Palestine*, Said traces the shift from a "liberation" struggle to a "nationalist" effort (163). Said uses the term "revolutionary" interchangeably with liberation. He notes, for instance, regarding the Nasserist and Baathist "inevitable" acceptance of the UN resolution 242 underlying worldview, that "Palestinian arms were less likely to be revolutionary than they were to be the arms of a state in the making" (163–164). Then, Said writes, that "during the post-Karameh period the Palestinian movement alternated between revolutionary vision and practical nationalist maneuvering" (164). Said's discussion about "complete liberation" (169) versus national independence crucially situates such distinctions in the historical context of the Cold War era. In this sense, the term "liberation" referred to "anti-imperialist" struggle (163, 168), whereas "national independence" euphemistically

Rhetorical History of Zionism's Third Persona

Zionism is often defined as Jewish national self-determination and the right to exist as a state in the Judaic biblical *Eretz Yisrael* or Land of Israel. While this definition might imply a type of neutral consensus, the story of Zionism is far from such. Today, there is a shift happening in American discourse and among some Israeli Jews about how to understand Zionism and the oppression of Palestinians. While many have long argued that Zionism is a violent project of settler colonialism,[7] other scholars and activists are beginning to realize that there are not two purported regimes between a democratic Israel and a temporary military occupation (Gaza, the West Bank, and East Jerusalem), but rather one regime from the Jordan River to the Mediterranean Sea that constitutes apartheid, a crime against humanity.[8] In a similar vein, the rhetorical genealogy of Zionism's Third Persona—the policy of Palestinian erasure—shows that one regime of Greater Israel, dependent upon the ethnic cleansing of Palestinians in order to

---

meant "political accommodation with the United States, respect for the integrity of each state in the area, and limited political objectives, all of them indicating acceptance (where there had once been refusal) of Israel" (168). Said notes that then-Egyptian President and anti-imperialist Gamal Abdel Nasser made this ideological shift after the 1967 War before he died in 1970, from anti-imperialist liberation to atomized Arab nationalisms.

[7] For example, see Abu-Lughod, "Imagining Palestine's Alter-Natives: Settler Colonialism and Museum Politics"; Bashir and Busbridge, "The Politics of Decolonisation and Bi-Nationalism in Israel/Palestine"; Busbridge, "Israel-Palestine and the Settler Colonial 'Turn': From Interpretation to Decolonization"; Halper, *Decolonizing Israel, Liberating Palestine: Zionism, Settler Colonialism, and the Case for One Democratic State*; Jong, "Zionist Hegemony, the Settler Colonial Conquest of Palestine and the Problem with Conflict: a Critical Genealogy of the Notion of Binary Conflict"; Khalidi, R., *The Hundred Years' War on Palestine: A History of Settler Colonialism and Resistance, 1917–2017*; Khalidi, W., *All That Remains: The Palestinian Villages Occupied and Depopulated by Israel in 1948*; Masalha, "The Palestinian Nakba: Zionism, 'Transfer' and the 1948 Exodus"; Pappé, "Zionism as Colonialism: A Comparative View of Diluted Colonialism in Asia and Africa"; Rouhana, "Decolonization as Reconciliation: Rethinking the National Conflict Paradigm in the Israeli-Palestinian Conflict"; Sa'di and Abu-Lughod, *Nakba: Palestine, 1948, and the Claims of Memory*; and Said and Hitchens, *Blaming the Victims: Spurious Scholarship and the Palestinian Question*; Sayegh, "Zionist Colonialism in Palestine (1965)"; Svirsky and Ben-Arie, "Settler Colonialism and the Logic of Double Elimination"; Todorova, "Reframing Bi-Nationalism in Palestine-Israel as a Process of Settler Decolonisation"; Veracini, *Israel and Settler Society*; and Wolfe, "Settler Colonialism and the Elimination of the Native."

[8] Legal definitions of apartheid include the 1973 United Nations International Convention on the Suppression and Punishment of the Crime of Apartheid which defines apartheid as "inhuman acts committed for the purpose of establishing and maintaining domination by one racial group of persons over any other racial group of persons and systematically oppressing them" (4), and the 2002 Rome Statute of the International Criminal Court that defines the crime of apartheid as inhumane acts "committed in the context of an institutionalized regime of systematic oppression and domination by one racial group over any other racial group or groups and committed with the intention of maintaining that regime" (4).

establish and maintain itself as such, was the endpoint for political Zionism since its inception and continues 125 years later. The genealogy of Zionism's Third Persona illustrates the ways in which Palestinian erasure is built into the foundation of Jewish ethnonationalist discourse of identity as a key mechanism to justify the discriminatory violence required to uphold its hegemony.

From a Jewish Zionist perspective, Zionism is a liberation movement that secures the safety and national self-determination of the Jewish people after millennia of persecution. Public intellectual and historian Arthur Hertzberg contextualizes the germination of Zionist ideology in the late eighteenth century when Jews in France were granted full citizenship rights after the French Revolution. This was the dawn of the era of emancipation in nineteenth-century Western Europe that would dramatically alter the heretofore-segregated role of internal Jewish life toward liberal ideas of universal humanity and civic participation in larger society. While Hertzberg begins the story of Zionism with emancipation in 1789, as an ideology and movement it would not gain traction until the late 1800s, about one hundred years later. Zionism, as it would come to be, was at the time incompatible with emancipation for Western European Jewry and Eastern European and Russian Jewish hopefuls who were concerned with the project of refashioning themselves as proper liberal citizen subjects in the drama of Western civilization's Enlightenment narrative. However, from the perspective of its European Jewish authors and advocates, this one-hundred-year period would prove to be a crucial precursor for the exigency and evolution of Zionist ideology, culminating in such breakthrough texts as Leon Pinsker's 1882 *Auto-Emancipation* and Theodor Herzl's 1896 *The Jewish State*.

Conceptually, the Jewish modern period laid the grounds for Zionism by reformulating religious tradition in secular terms. This reformulation establishes the conditions of possibility for the intertwining of Jewish religious and cultural identity with Zionist political ideology. As a way to accommodate emancipation, otherworldly pious beliefs—such as, God's covenant with the Jewish people, the Jewish nation as a holy community (or *Am Yisrael*, the People of Israel), and exilic return to Jerusalem—were translated into this-worldly secular terms.[9] Reform Judaism arose out of this context, in part as an attempt to reconcile Jewish commitment to *mitzvot* (God's commandments) alongside what seemed to be in contradistinction to secular state law. Hertzberg argues, "Nay more, the Messiah was now to be identified with the vision of an age of individual liberty and universal peace—i.e., with the progressive faith of the first half of the nineteenth century." Hertzberg demonstrates how the pious belief in waiting for and bringing about the Messiah was translated into secular values of legal emancipation. He further argues that the Reform Jewish movement revised its liturgy and omitted prayers for the otherworldly return to Zion in fear of misinterpretation that Jews were more loyal in a modern nationalistic sense to Jerusalem than to their home state in Europe (*The Zionist* 23).

In the mid-1800s, French Jewish philosopher Moses Hess (1812–1875) published *Rome and Jerusalem* that advocated for a Jewish socialist commonwealth in Palestine. Although there were preliminary signs of rising antisemitism, at the time Hess' proto-Zionist ideas were ignored since many of his contemporaries were still concerned with and had hope for equal inclusion as individuals in their home European countries. Israeli political scientist Shlomo Avineri argues, "The same criticism of bourgeois society which made Hess a socialist also convinced him that only a national home in Palestine could provide an adequate solution to the plight of the Jews, which was both a national and a socialist problem" (40). Around the same period, and in response to growing nationalisms surrounding and affecting their communities, Sephardic Rabbi

---

[9] See Rabkin, *A Threat from Within: A Century of Jewish Opposition to Zionism* for a provocative analysis of the way that Zionist political ideology appropriates Jewish religious tradition.

Judah ben Solomon Chai Alkalai (1798–1878) and Prussian Rabbi Zvi Hirsch Kalischer (1795–1874) called for Jewish resettlement in Palestine based on an activist attitude to redemption instead of what was perceived as passively waiting (50–51). Similar to Hess, Alkalai and Kalischer ultimately had little influence among their contemporaries or coming Zionist leaders such as Pinsker, Herzl, and Ahad Ha'am (Hertzberg, *The Zionist* 32).

Palestinian Arabs were also grappling with the apparent tension between religious belief and modern life in the second half of the nineteenth and early twentieth centuries. Palestinian education and law in the Ottoman Empire underwent drastic changes from traditional Islamic schooling and Sharia courts to secularized laws and educational curricula of math, science, and foreign languages, alongside rapid development of the railway, steamship, and telegraph. Following this period of Tanzimat reforms (1839–1876), the era of Sultan Abdul Hamid II's absolute rule began in 1876 and ended with the Young Turk Revolution of 1908. Initially Abdul Hamid II promoted the Ottoman Constitution of 1876, and this was taken as a sign of his belief in democratic rule. However, while he supported modernization in schools and industry, Abdul Hamid II quickly adopted a pan-Islamist policy in opposition to what he saw as Western intervention in Ottoman affairs and revoked the short-lived Constitution and Parliament in 1878 in reaction.

For Palestinian society, the exponential growth of new secular curricula in education stood in contrast to increasing Hamidian despotism; in retrospect Abdul Hamid II was inadvertently contributing to the conditions that would make possible his own deposition. Historian Johann Büssow writes, "In the 1880s, the Ottoman government began to perceive schools as key institutions for the future of the Empire." Citing historian Benjamin Fortna, Büssow argues that such perceptions "produced unanticipated consequences" that reinforced revolutionary ideas and in effect created a "politically conscious counter-elite" (68). Similar to

Palestinian intellectual and historian Rashid Khalidi's *Palestinian Identity*, Büssow shows how

the contradiction between absolute power and constitutional freedoms in effect facilitated

significant changes in Palestinian and Arab identity at the turn of the twentieth century. Studies

of autobiographies by young men from this period show that they prized their modern educations

as signs of advancement and progress in contrast to a "barbaric age" (58).[10] Modern Jewish

thinkers and early Zionists in Europe at this time held similar views that contrasted modernity

with tradition, positing the "Old World" as backwards and inferior, and associating 2,000 years

of exile with passivity, weakness, and poverty.

The rise of romantic nationalist movements across Europe set the stage for Jewish

assimilation and its failures, leading to the prejudicial "Jewish Question" or the "Jewish

Problem"—that is, the idea of Diaspora Jewry as an alien nation among nations, unable to fully

assimilate due to the fact of being a Jew, as a type of inborn pariah. This logic can be seen in

antisemitic conspiracies about the international Jew with perverse motives for "plotting against

society" (Hertzberg, *The Zionist* 61). The 1848 romantic nationalist movements, in reaction to

dynastic traditions of hegemonic power, would redraw the map of Europe in widespread calls for

national self-determination. From liberalism and legal equality (among men) grew particular

nationalisms with romantic mythologies of rugged individualism, glorified national pasts, and

deeply felt cultural attachments to language, land, and ethnic custom. Rather than Jewish failures

at full assimilation, Hertzberg points to Hess who foresaw that "racism would be more than

---

[10] For instance, young Palestinian men such as lawyer, politician and ethnographer 'Umar al-Salih al-Barghuthi (1894–1965) saw "contradictions between modern science and Islamic teachings" and became highly critical of totalitarian rule be it the Sultan or their own family fathers (Büssow 58). In his autobiography, educator and politician Ruhi al-Khalidi (1864–1913) "contrasted the respect for knowledge and freedom in the West with the ignorance and oppression that prevailed in the East" (Khalidi, *Palestinian* 79-80).

strong enough to prohibit the integration of the Jew as individual into the various national societies" (*The Zionist* 38). Purported scientific claims about national purity, biologically determined race, and racial superiority coincided with modern discourses of antisemitism and other virulent forms of racism such as Orientalism with regard to peoples throughout North Africa, the Middle East, and East Asia. Whereas previous anti-Jewish hatred and violence through the ages was based primarily on religious discrimination (and could be "solved" through forced conversion to Christianity albeit with continuing suspicion and surveillance), the logic of modern antisemitism viewed Jews as an inherently deviant biological race.

Nineteenth-century emancipation set the stage for Zionist rhetoric in the way that it reconfigured otherworldly terms of Jewish religion into this-worldly secular images, which further entailed a dramatic reinvention of Jewish self-understanding in such terms.[11] In contrast, pious Jews saw nationalist patriotic expression as a form of idol worship, and secular law as a heretical ideal. In *Imagined Communities*, political scientist Benedict Anderson opens chapter two with the tomb of the Unknown Soldier, an icon of national worship as it were. Anderson asks, what is it about nationalism (as a cultural artifact) that so many millions of people are willing to die for its cause? He argues that in Western Europe, "the eighteenth century marks not only the dawn of the age of nationalism but the dusk of religious modes of thought. … What then

---

[11] However, Zionist ideology would eschew *gezerah*, one particular aspect that Hertzberg argues Jewish tradition maintained through emancipation. In the exilic tradition, Jews typically viewed politically precarious situations and whatever changes in relationships with respective rulers through the lens of *gezerah*, "a destiny to be accepted with resignation." Hertzberg contends that in so doing, Jews would not break the Law of Torah. He writes, "In the here and now, the Jew is to allow nothing to stand between him and his full duty and devotion to the state which has emancipated him, but in the realm of faith he will maintain the concept of his chosenness and his dream of the Messiah" (*The Zionist* 22). Medieval Jewish history is a commonly evoked example of *gezerah* when, under the threat of expulsion, torture, and death during the varied Crusades in the Middle Ages and the Spanish Inquisition in 1492, Jewish families would go through the motions of conversion to Christianity and attend mass every week in order to survive. See works such as Chazan, *In the Year 1096: The First Crusade and the Jews* and *Daggers of Faith: Thirteenth-Century Christian Missionizing and Jewish Response*; and Graizbord, *Souls in Dispute: Converso Identities in Iberia and the Jewish Diaspora, 1580-1700.*

was required was a secular transformation of fatality into continuity, contingency into meaning"

(11). Without religious faith, the coincidence of birth and the chance of death seemed arbitrary

and random. The idea of the nation as such became a way to address transcendence in terms of

metaphysical immanence, to fulfill life's purpose in service of national ideals, and render

knowable the unpredictable through the power of reason.

The Beginning of Third Persona in Political and Cultural Zionisms

While Jewish exilic tradition saw emancipation as a *gezerah*,[12] plenty European Jewry

believed in and upheld liberal modernity in highest esteem, striving for the "heretical ideal."

Seminal Zionist figures like Leon Pinsker (1821–1891) and Theodor Herzl (1860–1904) believed

deeply in the promise of emancipation that European Jewry would be accepted and included in

enlightened modern society as men among equals, once and for all resolving the perennial

Jewish Problem. Henceforth, antisemitic backlash such as the 1881 Russian pogroms for Pinsker

and the 1894 Dreyfus affair in France for Herzl came as incredible mental and emotional shocks

to their liberal beliefs, transforming them from European integrationists into resolute Zionists.

Herzl had not yet read Pinsker's 1882 *Auto-Emancipation* before publishing his own

Zionist manifesto that promulgated a kindred analysis of antisemitism and Jewish national self-

determination (Hertzberg, *The Zionist* 43–44). Both saw Zionism as a solution to the Jewish

Problem because not only would it allow Jews to live as an equal nation among other modern

nation-states but it would also relieve those states "of its indigestible Jews." In this sense, Herzl

is known to have visited heads of state who were antisemitic but who might support Zionism

since it would help incentivize Jews to leave their European countries (47–49). At the time, this

rhetorical use of antisemitism in support of the Zionist cause made complete sense to Herzl, who

---

[12] See footnote 10.

was simultaneously disaffected with the misanthropy of legal emancipation's failed promises and energized with a manic impulse to write and advocate on behalf of a Jewish state. Pinsker and Herzl each believed that "Jew-hatred would persist as long as the mass of Jewry lived within non-Jewish majorities. […] Perforce, the world will have to answer its own problem in the only conceivable way, the territorial concentration of the Jews" (50–51).

European Jewish immigration to and Zionist settlement in Palestine began in the late 1800s and continued through several waves into the twentieth century. Rhetoricians Robert C. Rowland and David A. Frank argue that Zionism was a logical response to "the twin threats of loss of identity [through assimilation] and anti-Semitism" (*Shared Land* 39). Political scientist Joseph Massad does not see Zionism as a logical response to the twin threats of antisemitism and assimilation but rather as perpetuating those very problems. Massad argues that antisemitism is the epistemological ground upon which Zionism constructs its logic, aims, and actions. While Rowland and Frank examine the mythical potency and influential power of Zionist rhetoric to inspire *aliyah* (Jewish immigration to Palestine), Massad contends that "the very image of the Jews as carrier of European gentile civilization to a barbaric geography was definitional of Zionist political argumentation" (170). As emancipation in Europe proved unattainable for Jews, Massad critically argues that Zionism's desire for Europeanness (for that which it is rejected by) unfolded in a pervasive campaign against the Arab Other. Thus, Massad writes, "Zionism understood well that, for Jews to become European, they could not remain identified in tribal or religious terms, but rather in terms of race and nationhood" (169). In this way, Zionist ideology formulated Jewish identity in terms of race and nation through the new science of statistical demography, the modernization of Hebrew into a vernacular language, and the retelling of Jewish biblical narrative into a formal Zionist history of triumph over tragedy. As Zionism reconfigured Jewish national identity as such, Zionist rhetoric objectified the Arab Other in tribal and religious terms, in what Massad argues is precisely the same derogatory language that had been used against Jews in Europe in antisemitic epithets (172).

The early Zionist movement disavowed the existence of an Arab majority in Palestine and advocated for the proactive "ingathering of exiles" in the Land of Israel. In Pinsker's pamphlet *Auto-Emancipation*, this advocacy is implied in the title itself—that the Jews must not passively wait for permission from gentile society to be emancipated but instead take action to liberate themselves. Avineri argues, "To Pinsker, what Exile ultimately meant was to deprive the Jews of their active role in history" (78). Zionism believed that a type of secular repentance for the passivity and weakness associated with exilic tradition could be found in working the soil of *Eretz Yisrael* (the Land of Israel) in Palestine. The denigration of "Old World" Jewish diasporic tradition would become an especially prominent feature of Socialist Zionism among Eastern European and Russian Jewish settlers of the Second Aliyah (1904–1914) and in the rhetoric of David Ben-Gurion (1886–1973) who would become the first Prime Minister of Israel in 1948.

Akin to other romantic nationalist movements that glorified their past, Zionist rhetoric recast the revolts of Antiquity (such as, the Maccabean Revolt and Bar Kokhba Revolt) into triumphalist narratives that linked modern day struggle to a heroic lineage of righteous ancestors. Such triumphalism stood in direct contrast to 2,000 years of exile that were shunned in disparaging terms.[13] Historian Yael Zerubavel contends, "The Zionist binary model of Jewish

---

[13] Historian Yakov M. Rabkin argues that Jewish exilic framing of earthly events such as the destructions of the First and Secons Temple in Jerusalem is understood as a type of punishment for straying from God and the commandments, and for hatred among fellow Jews. Zionist secular interpretation turns this framing on its head and regards religious passivity as the reason for the Temple's destruction. Rabkin argues that the Zionist narrative "resorts to using history for its own ends, appropriating the Maccabees or Bar Kokhba, whom they transform into romantic resistance fighters against the foreign invader. The Zionist use of history is at the same time a rejection of the rabbinical interpretations, [and their] moral of the story is also opposed to the Jewish tradition: the Jews should have fought harder and better." According to this frame, military heroism and the new "brawny, strong-arm Hebrew" man is the only way to protect the Jews from antisemitic annihilation (69, 100). Rabkin contends that this

history portrays Antiquity as a positive period, contrasted with a highly negative image of Exile.

Since the main criterion for this classification is the bond between the Jewish people and their

land, the period of Exile is essentially characterized by a lack" (17–18). Whereas Eastern

European Zionists tended to emblematize sowing and the sickle in conjunction with biblical

rhetoric of redemption, Western European Zionists such as Herzl emphasized the advanced

technology and European civilization that the Jews would bring with them to what they saw as

an outdated Palestine. Despite these differences, both dominating perspectives sought statehood,

and portrayed Palestine as a desolate, neglected place with dilapidating villages and a nomadic

illiterate Arab population. Thus, it was, "A land without a people for a people without a land."[14]

However, not all early Zionist leaders believed that Jewish self-determination

necessitated the creation of a modern nation-state, or that Palestine was an empty, barren land.

Asher Zvi Ginsberg (1856–1927), primarily known by his Hebrew name Ahad Ha'am (meaning

"one of the people"), was a Russian Jew who drew upon Enlightenment philosophies such as

metaphysics of immanence to advocate for an agnostic spiritual Zionism, which sought to

establish a vibrant Jewish minority in Palestine as a way to inspire a Jewish cultural spiritualism

and reinvigorate the Hebrew language in modern spoken form.[15] He believed that although an

independent Jewish state in Palestine could be an eventual outcome, it was not required;

---

is the very thing that anti-Zionist religious Jews warn against: the use of force and a hastened return to *Eretz Yisrael* en masse is ultimately a transgression (a show of force of man's will over God's will) that will result in yet another exile.

[14] Despite the fact of a significant indigenous Arab majority already residing in and connected to the land in Palestine, "A land without a people for a people without a land" was a common Zionist slogan at the turn of the century, along with another popular slogan "make the desert bloom." Rabkin argues that Zionism "effaced and in fact refused to recognize the Arab presence in Palestine. In their enthusiasm, the Zionists would describe the flora and fauna around them in minute detail, while ignoring the Arab villages and their inhabitants" (65). By portraying the land as barren and empty as its premise, the slogans in effect justified Zionist colonization of the land. Put another way, the indigenous Arab population was not seen as fully human and thus blended into the landscape itself.

[15] In his view of cultural Zionism, Ahad Ha'am envisioned the formation of a vital Jewish minority in Palestine that would serve as the center of the Jewish world, emanating a refreshed spiritual tradition and unique set of values into the periphery of the Jewish majority in the diaspora and, "ultimately, for all humanity" (Hertzberg, *The Zionist* 71).

prioritizing political power would corrupt what he saw as the incumbent focus on the spiritual if statehood became the end goal of Zionism as Pinsker, Herzl, and others saw fit.[16] Not only did Ahad Ha'am speak out against political power as both a means and an end, but also controversially argued that "even a total concentration of Jewry in Palestine could not solve the Jewish problem" (Hertzberg, *The Zionist* 56). Furthermore, Ahad Ha'am insisted on gradualist growth of a minority and future establishment of a binational federation whereas state-based Zionism called for a swift ingathering of the majority and total political independence.

As a historical figure, Ahad Ha'am's outspokenness about the Arab majority and the challenges for Zionist settlement in Palestine would generate an alternative pathway for dissenters to follow. He not only offered alternative conceptions of Zionism apart from political, state-based interests, but was also one of the first on record from within the movement to discredit the claim that Palestine was a desolate land. In his 1891 essay "Truth from Eretz Israel," Ahad Ha'am writes about a myriad of concerns facing Jewish settlers. Famously, he states: "From abroad, we are accustomed to believe that Eretz Israel is presently almost totally desolate, an uncultivated desert, and that anyone wishing to buy land there can come and buy all he wants. But in truth it is not so" (full translation in Dowty, "Much" 161). Historian Alan Dowty calls attention to the fact that, while Ahad Ha'am makes powerful statements of acknowledgement given common claims to the contrary, the native Palestinian Arab population

---

[16] Ahad Ha'am observed two types of nationalism, one of political power exemplified among European states and two, what he saw as "the nationalism of the spirit, a unique genus of which there is only one species, the Jewish" (Hertzberg, *The Zionist* 55). Although Ahad Ha'am was agnostic, he drew upon religious history of the Prophets to expound his notions of modern spiritual Zionism. Commonly cited are his extrapolations from the Pharisees, a social movement and school of thought from 167 BCE to 73 CE during Second Temple Judaism in Jerusalem. Avineri argues, "The Pharisees, according to Ahad Ha'am, were the true synthesis of the spiritual with the material, and hence their dialectical defense of political power was viewed as a necessary tool but not as an end in itself" (126).

was not the central concern. Rather, Ahad Ha'am viewed "the Arab problem" as one hardship among many to be overcome.[17]

While dominant Zionist ideology fervently sought self-affirmation in light of the New Hebrew Hero through symbolism of the sickle and sword, both political and spiritual Zionism tended to deal with the native Palestinian Arab majority and its nascent nationalism in one or a combination of two ways: through outright denial, or, by regarding them as having a traditional culture in need of the modernization that European Jewish settlers would bring. The refusal to acknowledge the existence let alone the political will of native Palestinian Arabs was pervasive among Zionists. By 1922, Jews made up eleven percent of the total population in Palestine. Between the First Aliyah (1882–1903) and Second Aliyah (1904–1914) about seventy-thousand Jews immigrated to Palestine where more than 2½ million Eastern European and Russian Jews immigrated to the United States between 1880–1920. Zionist ideology had some influence for those in the Second Aliyah, but not as much as is commonly assumed. Predominantly Russian émigrés, they were fleeing widespread antisemitism, such as anti-Jewish riots (for instance, the 1905 Kishinev pogrom) and economic hardship.[18]

Despite being a small minority out of the larger Arab population in Palestine, Zionist leaders continued to ignore, deny, or downplay the significance of a people already living there who were calling Palestine their homeland for hundreds of, if not over thousands of years.[19] Zerubavel asserts, "The Zionist suppression of positive aspects of exilic life to promote the centrality of the people-land bond was reinforced by its denial of centuries of Palestinian life in

---

[17] Regardless, Dowty argues, "To be sure, in 1891 Ahad Ha'am did see beyond what others saw. He saw the Arabs not simply as passive objects of manipulation by others, but as actors with their own desires and aims. ... He also never claimed that Eretz Israel was 'an abandoned land', a phrase that occurs with regularity elsewhere in Zionist writings of the period" ("Much" 157).

[18] The question of whether Jewish immigrants to Palestine and then the State of Israel were immigrating due to antisemitic dispossession or for Zionist commitments remains a controversy in Israeli society.

[19] See Masalha, *Palestine: A Four Thousand Year History.*

that land" (22). In their analysis of the Zionist slogan "make the desert bloom," Rowland and

Frank similarly conclude, "But it [Zionist ideology] did not provide useful tools for dealing with

the indigenous population. In fact, it denied the existence of that population" (*Shared Land* 31).

Public intellectual Edward Said writes, "Far from the Arab multitudes signifying an already

inhabited land, to the early Zionist colonists these people were to be ignored" (*The Question* 18).

Said argues that the disavowal of Palestinian Arabs integral to Zionist colonization policy was

first formally codified in the 1917 Balfour Declaration, but seen earlier in artifacts such as

Herzl's *Diaries* (*The Question* 18-19).[20] Furthermore, in order to acquire land and settle in

Palestine, early Zionists dealt and negotiated with Arab absentee landlords, Ottoman officials in

Constantinople, and soon the authorities in Great Britain and the Hashemite dynasty, but never

with the Palestinian Arabs themselves who lived there. In this way, Zionism's Third Persona

becomes a failure of address that excludes the Palestinian Arab community—the "audiences not

present, audiences rejected or negated through the speech and/or the speaking situation" (Wander

209).[21]

---

[20] The Balfour Declaration issued by the British government is the first instance of formal codification that authorized the aims of political Zionism. For Zionist Jews, this was seen as a triumph and momentous accomplishment; for Palestinian Arabs, it was a complete betrayal. Zionism's Third Persona is built in the Declaration, which only refers to the native Arab population by who they are *not*, with the phrase "existing non-Jewish communities in Palestine." Senior Fellow at the Middle East Institute Khaled Elgindy argues that although the Declaration was indeed controversial among both U.S. government officials and in the American Jewish community at the time, "the Balfour Declaration became the primary lens through which American politicians viewed Palestine, the Zionist project, and Palestine's Arab inhabitants" (19). Elgindy analyzes transcripts from "a rather remarkable" 1922 congressional hearing with the Foreign Affairs Committee of the U.S. House of Representatives regarding a joint resolution endorsing the Balfour Declaration. In this hearing, "Palestine was described as a 'devastated and sparsely settled land', a country that was 'underdeveloped and underpopulated' with 'no civilization' to speak of. Meanwhile, Arab opposition to Zionism was attributed to ancient religious hatreds, outside agitators, or a stubborn resistance to 'civilization'" (19, 23).

[21] Said contends that despite Zionism's claims to moral high ground, the subjugation and silencing of Palestine's indigenous population was an inherent contradiction that would constitute Zionist and then Israeli state policy. He argues, "The fact is that 'Arabs' were always *being represented*, never able to speak for themselves" (*The Question* 25, *original emphasis*). Dowty suggests that this silencing was perhaps a coping mechanism for the Jewish settlers whose Zionist aspirations faced seemingly insurmountable obstacles. He writes, "For their own sanity, the new settlers needed to minimize the difficulties they faced and, in the case of the Arabs, it was also ideologically crucial to avoid any suggestion that they were simply replicating the Diaspora pattern of a Jewish minority existing at the sufferance of a majority non-Jewish host population." Moreover, Dowty contends, "The need to believe was

Palestinians continue to be Zionism's Third Persona, "a being whose presence, though relevant to what is said, is negated through silence" (Wander 210). This larger context of disregard and denial creates the exigency for Jewish rhetoric of dissent from within the Zionist movement both at the time and I argue as an ongoing legacy with regard to the State of Israel today. In this early context, simply the acknowledgement that a native Palestinian Arab population existed became a form of dissent, not to mention recognition of their national aspirations, full humanity, and equal rights.[22] These debates were multilayered, of course, where a common response to any acknowledgement of Palestinian Arab existence was an colonialist assertion (amply depicted in Herzl's 1902 utopian novel *Old New Land)* that the native

---

too strong and the full truth too threatening for most in the movement, as the earlier reaction to Ahad Ha'am's essay ['Truth from Eretz Israel'] had shown" ("A Question" 34, 37).

[22] See the remarkable dissenting speech by Yitzhak Epstein, "The Hidden Question," delivered in 1905 at the Seventh Zionist Congress and then published two years later in *HaShiloah* (a journal founded by Ahad Ha'am). Unlike "Truth from Eretz Israel," Epstein's "The Hidden Question" is entirely devoted to discussing Palestine's native Arab majority. Dowty contends, "Recognizing the collective dimension of Arab identity and interest, he [Epstein] laid down as one of his two basic principles that Zionists must respect not only individual rights, but also 'national rights.' In this respect Epstein was some seventy years ahead of the Zionist consensus" ("A Question" 36).

Epstein (1863–1943), a Russian émigré and Hebrew teacher, expressed grave concern regarding the Zionist strategy of acquiring Palestinian land via purchase from Arab absentee landlords and evicting native Arab peasants from the property they had been leasing for generations. From his personal experiences as a Jewish settler, Epstein recounts both the dangers and deep sadness in forcing Arab *fellahin* (peasantry) off the land, "whose grandfathers tilled the fields that they, their grandsons, are leasing" (full translation in Dowty, "A Question" 41). He writes, "this sale leaves in his heart a wound that will never heal, and he will always remember the cursed day in which his property fell into alien hands" (in Dowty, "A Question" 42). For Epstein, the eviction of Palestinian Arab *fellahin* was unethical, which he argued had to change in order to fulfill what he ultimately saw as Zionism's higher moral calling. In this way, Epstein destabilized Zionism's Third Persona. He states: "It must be admitted that up to now we had the 'wrong address'; in order to acquire our land, we turned to all the powers that had some link to it, we negotiated with all the in-laws but forgot about the groom himself: we ignored the true masters of the land" (in Dowty, "A Question" 51).

Palestinians were also speaking out about Zionist land purchases from Arab absentee landlords. During the Ottoman Constitutional Period from 1908–1914, the Arabic-language press flourished and created a type of counterpublic that investigated the Zionist movement and expressed opposition to it. Jewish immigration and Zionist land purchases were increasing with many immigrants staying past the expiration of their three-month permits yet reluctant to adopt Ottoman nationality (Khalidi, *Palestinian Identity* 120). Land sales and the dispossession of Palestinian Arab peasantry became one of the primary concerns for the newspapers' editors and writers. Newspapers such as *al-Karmil, Filastin,* and *al-Mufid* condemned the Arab absentee owners for selling the land to Jewish Zionist settlers, and "laid great emphasis on the importance of protecting the indigenous Palestinian peasantry from being expelled from its ancestral farmland to make way for colonists from Europe" (128). With a growing Palestinian nationalism and an increase in reports and editorials about the Zionist movement, this counterdiscourse understood that Zionists sought to displace native Palestinians and occupy their land, not to live with and alongside them.

population will be delighted and overwhelmed with all of the benevolent economic prosperity that the Jewish settlers will bring.

American Jews and Zionism

American Jews faced a dilemma with the Zionist demand that all Jews migrate to the Land of Israel. In other words, while a small but growing group of American Jews supported Zionism, they nonetheless remained in the U.S. From this nexus, U.S. Jewish Zionists needed to put their own "American" rhetorical twist regarding the debate of total ingathering of Jews in Palestine. Journalist and author John B. Judis pinpoints "a small minority of Reform Jews [who] played a very large role in creating an American Zionist movement" (137). There were American Jewish Zionists among Orthodox communities at the turn of the twentieth century, however secular and Reform Jewish leaders such as Richard Gottheil (1862–1936), Stephen Wise (1874–1949), Louis D. Brandeis (1856–1941), Judah Leib Magnes (1877–1948),[23] and Abba Hillel

---

[23] Historian Gideon Shimoni calls Judah L. Magnes "the quintessential dissenter" (374). Magnes was a California-born American Reform rabbi with a religiously conservative outlook; during his postgraduate work in Berlin from 1900–1902, he experienced the passionate debates between Zionists such as Chaim Weizmann, Martin Buber, Herzl, and others (Goren 11). He was particularly influenced by Ahad Ha'am's vision of Zionism as a way to reinvigorate and sustain Judaism in modern life, but unlike Ahad Ha'am's agnostic spirituality, Magnes' cultural Zionism was based in religious belief. Known for being his own version of a freethinker, Magnes criticized the Reform movement for "denationalizing" Judaism, while still upholding the Reform ethos of universal humanism (Goren 12). He rejected what he referred to as the "despair theory" of Zionism that saw the ingathering of exiles into territorial concentration as the only solution for Jewish survival. Historian Arthur A. Goren contends that for Magnes, "Palestine was the cornerstone, but the Jewish people would continue to live without it if need be and continue to develop its culture. However, 'with Palestine the people will live better, and develop its culture more hopefully and with more achievements', he insisted. 'We must help one another to be Jews and live as Jews, be it here or there'" (12–13). While Magnes had a decade of high influence in the American Jewish community from 1905–1915 as a young rabbi and magnetic orator from the pulpit in Brooklyn, New York, it was with the First World War that he became "the quintessential dissenter" and never looked back.

To the frustration of his family and at the risk of irreparable damage to some of his key relationships in the community, Magnes became a self-declared antiwar, anti-imperialist pacifist (Goren 23). When the historic Balfour Declaration was cause célèbre for many Jewish Zionists in 1917 (see footnote 19), Magnes dissented. In a 1920 personal letter to Norman Bentwich, British Zionist and Attorney-General of Mandatory Palestine, parts of which were later published in the *London Jewish Chronicle* and Magnes' *Like all the Nations?*, Magnes writes, "If self-determination if a just answer to other disputed problems, why not for Palestine and for the Jews? The fact is that Palestine has five or six times as many Arab inhabitants as Jews" (qtd. in Goren 187).

In his letter to Bentwich, Magnes warns, "This gift of political primacy to the Jews in Palestine rather than political equality contains the seed of resentment and future conflict" (qtd. in Goren 188). The reaction to Magnes' outspoken anti-imperialist dissent was difficult for him and his family; Goren contends, "Jewish leaders were dismayed over Magnes's political activities. ... His isolation from the Jewish community grew, and pressure

Silver (1893–1963) each had unique roles in both American politics and Zionist activism.

Despite such prominent leaders, in the first decade of the twentieth century, Zionism was not

widely accepted among American Jews, so many of whom were fresh arrivals fleeing from

antisemitism, and, somewhat akin to emancipation for Jews in Europe through the eighteenth and

nineteenth centuries, American Jews did not want to be seen as having dual loyalties when they

were trying to build lives in a new country.

Specific to this historical context, most American Jews at the time were anti-Zionist or

non-Zionist. Judis writes, "In Europe, being a Zionist meant wanting to *settle* sooner or later in

Palestine to build a Jewish state there. But few American Zionists contemplated moving to

Palestine. They had emigrated to the United States from Europe in order to escape anti-Semitism.

'America is our Zion', the Union of American Hebrew Congregations declared in 1898" (132,

original emphasis). What is today the Zionist Organization of America was originally founded in

1897 as the Federation of American Zionists (FAZ), which adopted a type of political Zionism.

Nonetheless, Richard Gottheil, president of FAZ, was adamant that Zionism did *not* mean, "'all

Jews must return to Palestine'" (Hertzberg, *The Zionist* 84). Wise expounded Herzlian notions of

---

mounted on him to withdraw from Jewish public life altogether" (26–27). With his wife Beatrice, Magnes decided to
move to Jerusalem in the early 1920s and for several years (until the 1929 Palestine riots) refrained from public
political advocacy. He put all his efforts toward founding Hebrew University with Albert Einstein, Chaim
Weizmann, and others, in his belief that the university could be an ideal place to foster Jewish-Arab understanding
and cooperation.

During his life Magnes published some two-hundred articles and addresses; the collection of Judah Leib
Magnes Papers in the Central Archives for the History of the Jewish People in Jerusalem includes about 2,600 files.
Goren writes that Magnes' wife, Beatrice, was "[a] woman of marked intellectual independence [and] a tower of
strength to her husband, helping him with her keen criticism of his ideas and plans" (14). She read the drafts of all
his articles. Magnes also exchanged drafts with colleagues at Hebrew University, including American-born Jewish
Zionist dissenter Henrietta Szold (1860–1945) who read the drafts of all his political articles (Goren xi, xiii). Judis
writes, "They [Magnes and Szold] advocated compromise between Zionism and Palestinian Arab nationalism—to
the disgust of American liberals like Wise, who thought Magnes was 'mad' and even 'treasonable'" (160). Szold
was the founder of Hadassah, the Women's Zionist Organization of America, and in 1942 along with Magnes,
Buber, and Ernst Simon, she co-founded Ihud (Unity), a political party that advocated for a binational one-state
solution with equal rights; Ihud's "journal, *Ner* (Candle), continued publication until 1964, thereby carrying the
small flame of Brit Shalom's moral-political tradition into the era of Jewish statehood" (Shimoni 374).

political Zionism[24] and, along with figures such as Brandeis, refashioned the ideology with an American patriotic emphasis. Wise and Brandeis argued that being American and Zionist was not a contradicting dual loyalty, but that Zionism itself was uniquely American (Judis 141).

Brandeis, who would become a U.S. Supreme Court Justice from 1916 to 1939, gave his famous 1915 speech "The Jewish Problem: How to Solve It" before a conference of Reform rabbis in New York, which advocated for the classic melting pot image of America as a nation of nationalities. Regarding the significance of this speech, Judis argues,

> But what about Zionism? Like other nationalities in America, Brandeis explained, Jews looked toward a home overseas—in their case, Palestine. In Palestine, Jews were trying to create a society based on democratic brotherhood. So, argued Brandeis, in being a Zionist and building a home for European Jews suffering from anti-Semitism, an American Jew was upholding the brotherhood of man. The American Zionist was fulfilling his responsibility as a Jew *and* as an American. (151, *original emphasis*)

There were tensions between American Zionists who stayed in the U.S. and European Jewish settlers in Palestine who firmly believed their American coreligionists should join them; regardless, the dominant strains of both parties supported the establishment of independent statehood despite their differences.

While, in general, American Jewish Zionists disagreed with settlers in Palestine regarding the total ingathering of exiles into territorial concentration, they also resisted the notion that Jewish life in *Eretz Yisrael* was naturally superior to that in the Diaspora. Mordecai Kaplan (1881-1983), whom Hertzberg refers to as one of "the most important of American Zionist thinkers," argued against the superiority complex by "continu[ing] to deny, root and branch, the

---

[24] When American Rabbi Stephen Wise met Herzl at the Second Zionist Congress in 1898 in Basel, Switzerland, it was life-changing for him.

notion that a significant Jewish life is impossible outside of the homeland" (*The Zionist* 90, 91).

Yet, due to geographic distance from Palestine and selective access to information about the land, American Zionists were in a sense worse off with regard to understanding the native Palestinian Arab majority who were still ninety percent of the population by the 1920s. Such high-ranking figures as Wise and Brandeis took Zionist rhetoric about a desolate Palestine at face value, in turn repeating this misrepresentation in their own advocacy. Judis argues, "In his speeches, Brandeis pictured Palestine as an empty room that Jews were entering. In his New York speech, he described Palestine as 'treeless and apparently sterile' and 'hopelessly arid' before the colonists arrived" (152–153). Thus, Zionism's Third Persona became integral to American Jewish Zionist rhetoric.

At first, Zionist discourse could justify settlement of the land because it denied anyone else lived there. As "the Arab question" gained visibility, Zionists, in congruence with the dominant Western colonialist mindset at the time, believed that the native population would happily accept the settlers' civilizing mission and "the question" would simply resolve itself. In their rhetoric, Wise and Brandeis drew direct historical comparisons between settlements in Palestine to America's early colonists in the sixteenth and seventeenth centuries, calling Jewish settlers in Palestine "pioneers" of Manifest Destiny. Similarly, European Jewish Zionist leader and statesman Chaim Weizmann appealed to these ideas in talks with British officials and in his frequent trips to the U.S. to lobby for the Zionist cause. Said argues that, in a 1918 letter from Weizmann to British Foreign Secretary Arthur Balfour, "Weizmann essentially recapitulates John Stuart Mill's arguments on representative government, by which the Indians were denied the right to rule themselves because they were centuries 'behind' the English" (*The Question* 28).

Put into practice, Zionism became both a form of settler colonialism and exclusionary ethnonationalism.

In addition to the colonialist logos, early American Zionists also—and perhaps more importantly to them—saw their support of Zionism as a way to charitably help their fellow Jews in Europe escape antisemitism. Wise and Brandeis were progressives who saw Zionism as an extension of their liberal beliefs. They were deeply immersed in political programs advocating for issues such as worker's rights, women's suffrage, and child labor laws; Wise became a cofounder of the National Association for the Advancement of Colored People and the American Civil Liberties Union. Judis writes, "They [Wise and Brandeis] wanted to aid the unfortunate. … And for many Jews, particularly Reform Jews, being a Zionist came to define and enliven Judaism for them. It displaced traditional observances as the focus of being Jewish" (132). Wise and Brandeis saw Zionism as a solution to the Jewish Problem, but still believed in a type of American exceptionalism for modern Jewish life distinct from the travails in Europe; the fatalistic estimate of antisemitism "did not apply to their own country" (Hertzberg, *The Zionist* 86). Even when the U.S. would not allow Jewish refugees in during or after World War II, American Zionists continued their lobbying efforts toward Palestine (Kaplan 25).

Jewish Statehood and Palestinian Rights

After the Holocaust, Israel's 1948 Declaration of Independence is depicted in Zionist mythos as a miraculous birth of a nation for the Jews. Yet, Israel's Independence was for Palestinians the 1948 Nakba (Arabic for catastrophe). From 1947–1949, more than 750,000 Palestinians were expelled[25] from their homes and between 400–600 Palestinian villages were

---

[25] Approximately 150,000 Palestinians remained in the areas of Palestine that became part of the Israeli state. Of the 150,000, about 40,000 were internally displaced. From 1948–1967, Palestinians in Israel lived under the strict surveillance of military law, which entailed the everyday survival and threat of brute force and further displacement; the survival and protection of Palestinian Arab identity and culture in an Israeli controlled

destroyed by Zionist paramilitary forces.[26] The Nakba became not a singular event but an

ongoing Zionist policy of Palestinian erasure. The collective memory and trauma of the Nakba

has and continues to shape Palestinian identity and everyday interpersonal relations. Historian

---

educational curriculum among extreme Israeli censorship of Palestinian print culture, media and literature (as well as simply what can be said aloud without being seen as a seditious threat); and it also entailed the overwhelming isolation from the rest of Palestinians outside of the Green Line in the Arab world. In addition to life under Israeli military law, the isolation from the Arab world contributed to a kind of double consciousness whereby fellow Arabs and Palestinians living outside of historic Palestine tended to see those who remained inside with the founding of the State of Israel as possibly accomodationist or collaborators with Zionist authorities. Caught in a double bind, Israeli authorities saw Palestinian citizens of Israel as seditious if they did not disavow their allegiance to or connections with Palestinians outside Israel or the larger pan-Arab community. Palestinians inside Israel then had to most carefully and critically navigate the terrain so as not to openly delegitimize the new Zionist state while at the same time not being perceived by their Palestinian and Arab compatriots elsewhere that they were thus being accomodationist or collaborative.

About Palestinians who remained in Israel after the Nakba, researcher Isabelle Humphries writes, "Fear of collaborators and informers successfully stifled most early political activity. ... Everyone was under suspicion. [...] The terror of speaking out became ingrained in a whole generation" (157). See Nassar, *Brothers Apart: Palestinian Citizens of Israel and the Arab World* for a history of the complex ways in which Palestinians in Israel upheld and transmitted Palestinian education and culture during this time, strategically navigating the double-bind dichotomy to resist and voice criticisms of the new Israeli state so as not to be read as an internal anti-Jewish threat, while still trying to remain connected and committed to Palestinian and pan-Arab history, literature, and community. Whereas the dominant Israeli frame positions Palestinian citizens as a possible seditious threat, the anticolonial Arab resistance movements viewed Palestinians inside Israel as reformist and accommodationist. Prominent Palestinian politician Shafiq Al-Hout reflects on this problem in his autobiography:

> As for those of our countrymen who remained in the territories occupied in 1948, they deserve our gratitude and recognition. Indeed we owe them our most sincere apologies for the harsh criticism we poured on them over the years because they decided to remain, steadfast and faithful, in their homes. We shunned them because they took Israeli citizenship, but today it is to them that we look for the prospect of liberating our land and restoring our rights. (82)

[26] Palestinian scholar Ghada Karmi's memoir *In Search of Fatima* offers a dispassionate yet heart-pounding account of the Nakba. She is eight or nine years old at the time growing up in Jerusalem, along with her big brother and their dog Rex. Chapter three opens up with the 1948 bombing of the Semiramis Hotel and her experience pinned against the wall with her family in their home, completely disoriented from terror and waking up in the middle of the night. After the Semiramis Hotel tragedy, Karmi recounts how the daily events worsen, culminating until she has to leave her home, Palestine, behind, along with Rex. *When to leave?* is the ultimate question that no one in her family wants to face.

Desperate to stay safe at home, Karmi's parents read the newspaper and listen to the radio intently for any promise. However, visits by friends and family slowly become less frequent. The butcher in the road closes down, and the ladies selling fruits, vegetables, and eggs stop coming by. Karmi wonders if anyone knew her family were still there. All the blinds and shutters get sealed shut. They start sleeping on the floor to safeguard themselves from the constant shootings and bullets flying through the air and in between houses. And then, the massacre at Deir Yassin happens, a village of roughly 600 people near Jerusalem, where Zionist paramilitary groups murder at least 107 Palestinian Arabs, including women and children. Women are raped and men, women, and children are tortured. News of Deir Yassin travels quickly into Jerusalem and all of the adults whisper the unspeakable. Deir Yassin becomes the breaking point for the women and children to leave, temporarily, until the war ends and they can return home. Karmi becomes overwhelmed and panicked as her mother packs up the house. The deep sadness, confusion, and helplessness of being forced to leave in fear of your life and family's safety turned to numbness as they waited for the fated taxi to arrive. Karmi, her brother, sister, and mother, all planned on returning to their home in Jerusalem, where their father remained as they drove away.

Rosemary Sayigh writes, "1948 was '*The* Event' that meant the beginning of a destiny of victimhood, and of tragedy to be repeated through further displacements and losses. […] The Nakba became a constituent of Palestinians' sense of identity not only because of the scale of their loss, but also because it generates new catastrophes that scar each succeeding generation afresh" (142, 153).[27] Repeated tragedies and further displacements include the 1967–present Israeli military occupation and Jewish settlement construction, the 1982 Sabra and Shatila massacre at Palestinian refugee camps in Lebanon, and since the turn of the twenty-first century, the 2008, 2012, and 2014 Israeli military operations that each time demolishes Gaza once more.

In its historical context, what I refer to as the American and Israeli shared frame, constituted through Zionism's Third Persona, merged in dominant discourse after the June 1967 Six-Day War. The Israeli victory in the 1967 War became a rallying cry of support by Jews in the Diaspora for the nascent state. Since this turning point, the dominant frame casts supporters and critics of Israel in an oppositional logic of "us versus them," or pro-Israel versus pro-Palestine. In the dramatic tension leading up to Israel's preemptive strike in June 1967, American Jews overseas looked on in unbearable fear of the possibility of Israel's destruction by the surrounding Arab armies that would result in a second holocaust. After Israel's sweeping victory, the mythic image of "David versus Goliath" with Israel as the underdog up against hostile Arab countries inscribed itself into the American Jewish psyche and "offered a folk theology of 'Holocaust and Redemption'" (Novick 150).

---

[27] Social scientists Ahmad H. Sa'di and Lila Abu-Lughod write about the Nakba as a mode of temporality that becomes the framework through which reality is understood and identity is constructed:

> The Nakba is often reckoned as the beginning of contemporary Palestinian history, a history of catastrophic changes, violent suppression, and refusal to disappear. It is the focal point for what might be called Palestinian time. … Moreover, it is the creator of an unsettled inner time. It deflects Palestinians from the flow of social time into their own specific history and often into a melancholic existence, … or a ghostly nostalgia. (5)

Historian Peter Novick argues that while American Jews supported Israel post-WWII particularly with regard to resettlement for Holocaust survivors and refugees, throughout the 1940s and 50s the Jewish victim symbol was "actively shunned." Novick contends, "As Israelis were 'negating' the Diaspora victim condition (very much including the Holocaust), American Jews, in a parallel fashion, regarded the victimhood symbolized by the Holocaust as a feature of the Old World that they, likewise, were putting behind them" (121). However, along with the outpouring of support after the 1967 war, Holocaust remembrance would come to intertwine with Israel advocacy in the mainstream American Jewish community.

Six years later with the 1973 Arab-Israeli War, the American and Israeli shared frame recalibrated Israel's victorious image into one of ongoing isolation in a hostile region of anti-Jewish neighbors. While this created a kind of contradiction it was nonetheless a successful rhetorical strategy for harnessing support of Israel for American Jewry. Novick writes,

> Illusions of Israeli invincibility and self-sufficiency were among the casualties of this war [1973 October War]. A related casualty was the contrast, traditionally drawn by Zionists, between the vulnerability of Jews in the Diaspora, culminating in the Holocaust, and the security that Jews could find in a Jewish homeland. Clearly there was no place in the world *less* secure for Jews than in Israel. (151, *original emphasis*)

In other words, while Holocaust-centered Zionist rhetoric continues to claim that Jews in the Diaspora need the State of Israel for Jewish security, Israel also frames its geopolitical position as constantly under antisemitic existential threat and attack. Regardless, for many Jews, the State of Israel represents a necessary place of safety and refuge.

Crucially, Jewish rhetoric of dissent interrogates the exclusionary ethnonationalist notion of Jewish safety and reframes Jewish security as bound up with the freedom and rights of all oppressed people. As I will show in chapters two, three, and four, Jewish dissenters utilize

rhetorical refusal and dissociative techniques to break the links in dominant discourse that attach

the threat of antisemitism to protectionist modes of ethnonationalist supremacy. At the heart of

this reinvention of identity, American Jewish dissenters reframe the threat of antisemitism *in

connection to* other forms of ethnic and racial prejudice, not uniquely separate from.

Antisemitism is a form of ethnic, racial, and religious prejudice and hatred toward Jews for being

Jews.[28] The question of antisemitism in and of itself is not up for discussion, which is on the rise

in the U.S., Europe, and throughout parts of the world.[29] Rather, I am interested in how

antisemitism gets interpreted and becomes embedded in the debate about Zionism and the State

of Israel and by extension, narratives of Jewish self-understanding.

In chapter two, I examine Zionism's Third Persona in the rhetoric of Holocaust-centered

existential threat. I focus on the rhetorical construction of dominant narratives around discourses

of Israel's right to exist and right to defend itself, and the ways that such discourses frame

Palestinian struggles for freedom in terms of terrorist threat (as the Third Persona). In chapters

two, three, and four, I present case studies of representative texts of Jewish dissent, including

Arthur Hertzberg, Peter Beinart, Sara Roy, and the activist groups IfNotNow and Jewish Voice

for Peace. I delineate a genealogy of dissent that reframes the Zionist myth of rebirth and

redemption. I show that there is a larger rhetorical corpus of American Jewish dissent that

---

[28] The Anti-Defamation League (ADL) defines antisemitism as: "The belief or behavior hostile toward Jews just because they are Jewish. It may take the form of religious teachings that proclaim the inferiority of Jews, for instance, or political efforts to isolate, oppress, or otherwise injure them. It may also include prejudiced or stereotyped views about Jews" ("Antisemitism").

[29] In their "Audit of Anti-Semitic Incidents: Year in Review 2018," the ADL reports: "2018 included the deadliest attack on Jews in the history of the U.S.: The massacre of 11 Jewish worshippers, and an additional two more injured, at the Tree of Life Synagogue in Pittsburgh by a white supremacist in October. The Pittsburgh attack was one of 39 reported physical assaults on Jewish individuals in 2018, a 105% increase over 2017. A total of 59 individuals were victims of assault, not including the police officers injured at the Tree of Life Synagogue." Also in her 2019 report "The Alarming Rise of Anti-Semitism in Europe," Human Rights Watch Researcher Eva Cossé states: "The evidence of rising anti-Semitism in Europe has become impossible to ignore."

employs first-person identity reconstitution and dissociative strategies to reframe dominant discourse about the unique threat of antisemitism to the State of Israel and reinvent identity in relation to Palestinian freedom and rights.

Chapter three examines first-person identity reconstitution as a transformative rhetorical resource in dissenting narratives concerning Jewish support for Palestinians' human rights. First-person identity constitution examines the ways in which authors and speakers constitute their identities in discourse through narrative about their personal realities. Influenced by rhetorician Kenneth Burke's alchemic opportunities for transformation and philosopher Judith Butler's modality of ethical relations, I argue that a critical rhetoric of first-person narratives can promote the formulation of an identity framework that can be utilized as an ethical practice in relation to alterity. In other words, identity is neither fixed nor final but an iterative process that can (re)orientate as an ongoing ethical practice. This effort is exemplified in the writings of Peter Beinart and Sara Roy, who are American Jewish dissenters that support Palestinian rights. In the process of speaking out, they have reinvented Jewish self-understanding apart from the dominant Zionist identity formations.

Chapter four looks at contemporary dissent around Zionism and the rhetorical refusal of birthright discourse through the lens of the universal audience as a definitional concept of identity. The universal audience becomes political because it constructs and advocates for certain conceptions of the real over others. As a dissociative strategy, rhetorical refusals can work to expose the ways in which hegemonic notions of universality depoliticize the political by naturalizing the status quo. Moreover, refusals reinvent who or what constitutes the universal audience by deliberately breaking with accepted protocol in an appeal to higher moral ground. This chapter performs a close reading of two political campaigns by American Jewish student activists who recast the ethnonationalist meaning of Jewish birthright to Israel through dissociative rhetorical moves. The dissenters' reinvented notion of birthright expands the universal Jewish audience as a definitional concept of identity to incorporate Palestinian rights. These features of their reinvented audience envision a binational rhetoric of belonging for both Israelis and Palestinians. This study of student activists' rhetorical refusal of birthright provides an important case for analyzing social justice protest strategies and their effects on ethnonationalist conceptions of the real.

In chapter five, I turn toward rhetoric and composition pedagogy. Based on my research of rhetorical refusal and audience in the Israel-Palestine conflict, I am interested in the practical application of teaching refusal in the writing classroom. Teaching rhetorical refusal can cultivate critical rhetorical awareness in students, particularly when it comes to what rhetorician Nancy Welch calls "questions of audience discernment" (306). The subtitle in *Rhetorical Refusals: Defying Audiences' Expectations* by rhetorician John Schilb also points to analytical concerns regarding audience discernment. Rhetorical refusals happen when the author or speaker deliberately breaks accepted protocol held by the audience in an appeal to higher moral ground. Schilb contends that refusals can "spark better reflection in their audiences than does the usual languages of politics" (178), and by studying such rhetorical refusals, I explore how it can also spark reflection in students. How can teaching rhetorical refusal develop students' awareness of power relations and audience discernment, both "real" audiences and audience as a construct of the author or speaker? In this final chapter, I offer a lesson plan based on Jewish student activists who refused maps of Greater Israel dispersed on Birthright trips that fail to demarcate the occupied Palestinian territories. What rhetorical work is the Greater Israel map doing? What rhetorical work are student activists engaging when they refuse such maps? Who is the audience

of this refusal and how does it spark reflection?

Chapter 2

Zionist Rhetoric of Existential Threat

In the larger context, misuse of antisemitism is integral to Israeli security propaganda: this is the rhetoric of existential threat that relies on the racist stereotype of the antisemitic Arab Islamic terrorist in order to justify Israel's military regime and subjugation of an entire people. Israeli Prime Minister Benjamin Netanyahu promotes this worldview and has been accusing human rights activists in Palestine of antisemitism for quite some time.[30] Misuse of antisemitism includes false allegations, character assassination, targeted smear campaigns against individuals, and guilt by association, all of which is disproportionately aimed at Palestinian scholars and solidarity activists.[31] Israeli Jews fighting for Palestinian rights have been smeared as terrorist sympathizers and traitors to the Jewish people.[32] Misuse of antisemitism is not only an attempt to stifle dissent and scare advocates into silence, but also becomes a tactic of distraction that takes time and resources away from addressing the issues of settler colonialism, military occupation, apartheid, and Palestinian freedom.[33]

---

[30] For example, see Black, "Israel boycott movement is antisemitic, says Binyamin Netanyahu"; El-Ad, "Netanyahu Exploits the Holocaust to Brutalize the Palestinians"; Heller, "Netanyahu accuses ICC of anti-Semitism in pursuit of war crimes probe"; and Zonszein, "Anti-Semitism doesn't bother Benjamin Netanyahu if it comes from his political allies."

[31] For example, see Kane, "A Pro-Israel Lawyer Is Weaponizing Public Records Law Against Palestinian Activists"; "Part III: Fighting False Charges of Antisemitism" in *On Antisemitism: Solidarity and the Struggle for Justice* edited by Jewish Voice for Peace; and Palestine Legal, "Backgrounder on Efforts to Redefine Antisemitism as a Means of Censoring Criticism of Israel."

[32] For example, see May, "Democratic Activists Are Now Marked Out as Israel's New 'Traitors'" and Shakir, "Amnesty International Staffer Challenges Israel's Travel Ban." Regarding Jewish criticism of Zionism and the modern day *herem* (excommunication), see Hahn Tapper, "Why is 'anti-Israel' the only cause for excommunication in American Judaism?"; Magid, "Butler Trouble: Zionism, Excommunication, and the Reception of Judith Butler's Work on Israel/Palestine"; and Trachtenberg, "The New Kherem, or 'Barry Trachtenberg Does Not Represent Us!': On speaking for and against Jewish self-interests."

[33] See Friedman, moderator, "Implications and Impacts of the IHRA Definition on Palestinians."

Antisemitism is traditionally defined as prejudice against Jews for being Jewish, and is manifested in stereotypes, conspiracy theories, hate speech, and physical violence. In 2016, the International Holocaust Remembrance Alliance (IHRA) adopted a framework of antisemitism that expands upon the traditional definition to include the targeting of Israel for criticism, such as claiming that the existence of the State of Israel is a racist endeavor.[34] In a recent statement with 122 Palestinian and Arab signatories, they write: "To level the charge of antisemitism against anyone who regards the existing state of Israel as racist, notwithstanding the actual institutional and constitutional discrimination upon which it is based, amounts to granting Israel absolute impunity" (Abdallah, et al.). Zionism is a form of exclusionary ethnonationalism that has resulted in anti-Arab racist policies including legal segregation from Jews and the ongoing dispossession of Palestinians from their land; millions of Palestinians live under Israeli military law with no citizenship status or civil rights.[35] However, in the framework of the IHRA definition, which conflates the Jewish people with the modern-day State of Israel, critics of such crimes can be accused of antisemitism.

---

[34] See the IHRA "Working Definition of Antisemitism" here: https://www.holocaustremembrance.com/resources/working-definitions-charters/working-definition-antisemitism

[35] Israeli Jewish settlers enjoy all the same privileges as citizens living within Israel proper, while their Palestinian neighbors do not have citizenship status or civil rights and instead live under Israeli military law. Living under military law, among other problems, systematically deprives Palestinians of rights such as the right to vote for the government that exercises state power over them. They are denied a voice or representation in policymaking and zoning laws. Israeli military law also constricts Palestinian mobility with roadblocks, checkpoints, and other barriers to movement, and authorizes Israeli confiscation of Palestinian land in order to build more Jewish settlements.

B'Tselem reported that from 2006 to 2018, Israel demolished at least 1,397 Palestinian residential units in the West Bank, causing 6,186 people—including at least 3,124 minors—to lose their homes ("Statistics on demolition"). Martial law justifies demolitions when Palestinians build homes without official Israeli permits to do so. However, with the few permits granted each year, it leaves many Palestinians no choice but to build without official authorization. In 2015 the United Nations reported that between 2010 and 2014, Palestinians in the West Bank submitted over two thousand applications for building permits to Israeli authority and only thirty-three (1½ percent) were approved ("Under" 4). B'Tselem argues that Israeli military law does "not take into account ... the history of Palestinian residence on the land (documented at least as far back as the nineteenth century) or the residents' independent ability to construct public buildings to serve the neighboring Palestinian communities." Conversely, the law has "granted the [Israeli Jewish] settlers substantial tracts of land for agricultural use and future development" ("The South").

As I discussed in chapter one, from the perspective of Jewish Zionists, Zionism is often defined as a liberation movement for Jewish national self-determination and the right to exist as a state in the Land of Israel (historic Palestine). In historical context, Zionism is Jewish ethnonationalism, a political ideology that began in Europe in the 1880s. Ethnonationalism, taken to its logical conclusion, believes in ethnic purity and supremacy and the right to statehood for the presumed homogenous group. Other iterations of ethnonationalist ideology include Turanism (Turkish nationalism), Hindutva (Hindu nationalism in India), Iranian nationalism, and white Christian nationalism in the United States. Ethnonationalist ideology is fear-based and motivated by an "anxiety of incompleteness" that underlies the drive for complete ethnonational purity (Appadurai 9).

Ethnonationalism can be inherently exclusionary and dangerous in the way that it seeks to create a homogenous ethnostate with a demographic majority. According to Israel's own rhetoric, for example, in order to be considered a *Jewish* state it must have Jewish demographic majority, what Israeli journalist Gideon Levy calls "Israel's 'Jewish Majority' Obsession." In addition to being seen as a terrorist security threat, Palestinians are also regarded as a demographic existential threat. Notwithstanding the millions of Palestinians in diaspora and in refugee camps in neighboring countries, *if Israel granted the five million Palestinians in the West Bank and Gaza Strip citizenship status and voting rights for the Greater Israel regime that rules over them, it would mean that Jews are no longer legally the demographic majority, which, according to ethnonationalist rationale, would destroy the Jewish character of the state.* As such, it is plain to see that the oft-heard phrase "Jewish and democratic" is antithetical because the exclusionary and violent project of maintaining a majority is fundamentally antidemocratic.

This chapter builds upon the rhetorical genealogy of Zionism's Third Persona from chapter one to show how Holocaust memory[36] and antisemitism are framed and deployed to reinforce the erasure of Palestinian history and life. The IHRA definition and the vast efforts of Israel advocates to codify it into law[37] is not a new controversy; rather, it is the culmination of decades of insistence that "anti-Zionism is the new antisemitism." In 2020, then-U.S. Secretary of State Mike Pompeo issued a statement saying, *"Anti-Zionism is anti-Semitism"* (@StateDept). Pompeo's statement echoes from a 1973 American Jewish Congress publication where Israeli politician Abba Eban said that "anti-Zionism is merely the new anti-Semitism" (qtd. in Weiss). As this chapter illustrates, the underlying goal of this equation is to render unfathomable Palestinian self-determination because Palestinian rights is seen as an existential threat to Israel. This is the analytical and deliberative task for Jewish dissenters: to reflect on white Jewish privilege with regard to Israel and present a counterdiscourse to Zionist rhetoric of existential threat so as to help render intelligible the Palestinian plight under Israeli domination.

I present a case study of Hertzberg's 1988 "Open Letter to Elie Wiesel" as a compelling dissociation that breaks the links of this equation in his recognition of Palestinian suffering. Hertzberg's letter establishes a significant departure from Zionism's Third Persona and carves out a path for Jewish dissent and reinvented identity to follow. In the context of post-1967

---

[36] For work on the Holocaust and the politics of memory, see the foundational text by Friedlander, *Memory, History, and the Extermination of the Jews of Europe*. For work on the Holocaust and the politics of memory in Israel, see Benbassa, *Suffering as Identity: The Jewish Paradigm* and Segev, *The Seventh Million: Israelis and the Holocaust*. For work on the Holocaust and the politics of memory in the U.S., see Flanzbaum, ed., *The Americanization of the Holocaust*; Lipstadt, *Holocaust: An American Understanding*; Magid, "The Holocaust and Jewish Identity in America: Memory, the Unique, and the Universal"; and Novick, *The Holocaust in American Life*. For critical work on reimagining historical consciousness, see Bashir and Goldberg, eds., *The Holocaust and the Nakba: A New Grammar of Trauma and History*. See Finkelstein, *Beyond Chutzpah: On the Misuse of Anti-Semitism and the Abuse of History* and *The Holocaust Industry: Reflections on the Exploitation of Jewish Suffering*, regarding the misappropriation of antisemitism and abuse of Holocaust history to justify Israeli war crimes against Palestinians.

[37] See Palestine Legal, "Legislation."

American Jewish identification with Israel and Holocaust memory, Hertzberg's open letter represents a key moment of dissent when dominant discourse insisted that Israel had no negotiating partner in the Palestine Liberation Organization (PLO), criminalized by the U.S. and Israel as a terrorist organization. Constituted by and through Zionism's Third Persona, the stereotype of the Jew-hating Arab terrorist becomes bound up with the rhetorical deployment of antisemitism and Holocaust memory as a way to normalize dominant notions of Israel's right to exist and defend itself. The condition of possibility for the normalization of Zionism and Israel, then, is the Nakba, the disappearance of Palestine. Because of this, dominant Zionist ideology operates through self-legitimating metanarratives such as the IHRA definition that exceptionalize antisemitism in order to both mask and morally justify the violence required for the creation and maintenance of the settler state.

As representative texts in this larger discourse, Wiesel's *New York Times* editorial and Hertzberg's response to it help to better understand the intertwining of these elements that reinforce Jewish ethnonationalist hegemony. While there were decisive American Jewish dissenters through the 1970s and 80s advocating for negotiations with the PLO, such as Noam Chomsky, Rabbis Arnold Jacob Wolf, Arthur Waskow, Henry Siegman, and Michael Lerner, in addition to the 1973–1977 group Breira: A Project of Concern in Diaspora-Israel Relations, I am interested in how Hertzberg's open letter to Wiesel fundamentally disrupts Zionism's Third Persona by articulating a Jewish rhetoric of identity as an ethical mode of relating to Palestinian alterity. In this way, Hertzberg opens a space of potentiality for cultural transformation.

The Antisemitic Arab Terrorist Other

In the 2015 anthology *Toward a Critical Rhetoric on the Israel-Palestine Conflict*, rhetoricians wrestle with the seemingly impenetrable pathos and its underlying historical traumas that continue to plague thoughtful deliberation about Israel about Palestine. In the first essay of the anthology, Anis Bawarshi looks to the function of memory and uptake as it contributes to the debate impasse. He writes, "Uptakes have memories in the sense that they are learned recognitions and inclinations that, over time and through ideological reproduction, become habitual. Our uptake memory is what we bring to a rhetorical encounter, and it is what helps us select from, define, and make sense of that encounter" (13). Uptake becomes a methodological tool to track and understand the ways in which rhetoric can enable reinvented meaning from preexisting intertextual and asymmetrical relations (Bawarshi, "Beyond" 246). Meaning is neither static nor fixed but constantly negotiated, reiterated and solidified, or open to a transposition of terms with each unfolding rhetorical situation. Uptake, then, does not focus on meaning inherent in an object but rather the ways in which an object gets taken up, utilized, and narrated for particular purposes as an address to target audiences.

For Zionism's Third Persona, the uptake of the antisemitic Arab terrorist Other occurs through a rhetorical strategy of decontextualization. The dominant Israeli frame suffers from a chronic absence of context, which works to position Palestinian armed struggle and collective resistance as atomized accounts of unprovoked antisemitic violence.[38] Such isolated incidents of what Israel frames as Palestinian terrorism then justifies Israel's use of brute force and military

---

[38] Communication and media studies scholars have produced analyses of how events in the Israel-Palestine conflict are reported and represented in English language journalism. See Barkho, "The Discursive and Social Paradigm of Al-Jazeera English in Comparison and Parallel with the BBC"; Dunsky, *Pens and Swords: How the American Mainstream Media Report the Israeli-Palestinian Conflict*; Friel and Falk, *Israel-Palestine on Record: How the* New York Times *Misreports Conflict in the Middle East*; Peterson, *Palestine-Israel in the Print News Media: Contending Discourses*; and Philo and Berry, *Bad News From Israel.*

violence. For instance, historian Seth Ackerman examines network TV's reporting of events at the beginning of the Second Intifada (2000–2005) among ABC, NBC, CBS, and CNN, and argues that "instead of an honest accounting of each side's grievances, journalists reporting the clashes in the West Bank and Gaza offer what is, in effect, a daily catalogue of seemingly unprovoked Palestinian aggression" (62). Dominant U.S.-Israel terrorism discourse relies upon a narrative strategy that continues to isolate events in a string of seemingly unexplainable anomalies of violence other than that of pure Arab hatred of the Jews. Within this frame, Palestinian resistance to Israeli occupation becomes an omniscient threat, a looming danger embodied by the homogenized Arab Other, to the security of the state. In this sense, the continuous uptake of atomized violence can only be explained by the perverse Arab desire to obliterate the State of Israel because it is a *Jewish* state, rather than an organized resistance movement in protest to Zionism's history of dispossessing Palestinians and occupying their land. When the Palestinian struggle for freedom is diagnosed as terrorism fueled by antisemitism, the larger context of Zionist colonization and Israeli military occupation becomes disavowed.

The dual strategy of decontextualization and omission of Palestinian self-representation perpetuates a sanitized version of Israeli domination that depicts Palestinian and Israeli narratives as two sides of a level playing field. Decontextualized accounts not only evade the reality of an overwhelming imbalance of power between Israeli citizens and stateless Palestinians. They also perpetuate Orientalist stereotypes of the one-dimensional Arab terrorist, in effect justifying the status quo of the occupation in the name of Israeli national security. Film theorist Dorit Naaman contends, "The discourse on terrorism ... effaces the root causes of political violence and prevents a sober discussion that explains (but does not necessarily justify) the historical and political reasons for such violence" (940). By neglecting context, the shared Israeli and

American dominant frame continues to narrowly portray Palestinian resistance as unprovoked aggression and religious fanaticism.

Rhetorician Michael Kleine calls the Israeli versus Palestinian framing of history and current events "extreme narratives" that suffer from narration sickness, a device from Paulo Freire that Kleine describes as "a monological pathology that exists because of the absence of dialog" (92). In the Palestinian and Israeli extreme narratives, the hero/villain binary is ascribed with the roles reversed, and the hero/villain monological pathology becomes one of the means through which violence is legitimized. Kleine argues, "Each side interprets events in terms of their own story, demonizes the other and omits their own contribution to the conflict. Each side is in a state of denial, ignoring the response to their own actions" (95). By situating the extreme narratives side by side, the narration sickness exposes itself. In addition to the hero/villain binary, decontextualization also enables the "clash of civilizations" narrative frame or "the 'cosmic struggle' argument, i.e., no side can be blamed for what is happening because the conflict has been going on since time immemorial for reasons that are beyond human comprehension" (Abraham, "Reluctant Rhetoricians" 33). Nonviolent protests for Palestinian rights far outweigh armed violence in sheer numbers; however, mainstream U.S. media sensationalizes violence, especially violence carried out by the Israeli frame's presupposed threat, the antisemitic Arab terrorist. This violence is hyper-sensationalized in a series of uptakes saturated with traumatic memory.

Holocaust-Centered Worldview and the Terrorist Threat

Holocaust memory has become bound up with reductionist for-or-against narratives, both in terms of outward perception of Jews to the broader public and particularly with respect to American and Israeli Jewish self-understanding. It is a lens or worldview through which current situations are interpreted. Dominant Zionist rhetoric and mythos regard the State of Israel's origin story as a miracle born from unthinkable devastation and unparalleled circumstance. Six million Jews were methodically murdered in concentration camps in Eastern Europe from 1941-1945, otherwise known by Nazi officials as the "Final Solution to the Jewish Question" policy of extermination. Just less than three years after the end of World War II, Israel declared national independence. For many Zionists who hold what Rowland and Frank refer to as "the myth of Holocaust and Redemption" (*Shared* 107) or a "Holocaust-centered worldview" (Rowland 120), a militarized homeland in the name of self-defense against the ever-present antisemitic existential threat of another holocaust was and remains the only answer. Political scientist Bashir Bashir and historian Amos Goldberg write, "The expression *meSho'ah le-tekumah* (from Holocaust to rebirth) became a constitutive slogan of Zionist consciousness, and it remains so to this day" (5).

Holocaust-centered Israeli security rhetoric is tied to the legacy of Menachem Begin (1913–1992), who was a leader of the Irgun paramilitary group in Mandatory Palestine, founder of the right-wing Likud political party in 1973, and sixth Prime Minister of Israel from 1977–1983. Begin is known for being a persuasive orator whose hardline Zionist ideology held no compromise in the name of Jewish national security. Rowland and Frank argue, "In this view [Begin's Holocaust-centered worldview], violence, even if it resulted in the death of innocent Palestinians, was needed to protect the Jews" ("Mythic" 47). Like his ideological predecessor Ze'ev Vladimir Jabotinsky (1880–1940) and present-day Likud party successor Benjamin Netanyahu, Begin was a territorial maximalist who believed all of the Land of Israel from the Jordan River to the Mediterranean Sea belongs to the Jews, known as Greater Israel.[39] Begin also

---

[39] Today, the Eretz Israel Caucus is one of the largest and most active groups in the Knesset that supports the State of Israel's indefinite control over the West Bank.

"placed ultimate responsibility for the Holocaust on Jewish weakness," and, through this worldview, argued that by becoming the New Hebrew Hero Jews can cleanse themselves of their own passivity and weakness. Within this narrative frame, the mythic Zionist hero does not simply defeat the anti-Jewish villain, but in so doing, redeems himself of survivor's guilt from the Nazi genocide (Rowland and Frank, "Mythic" 44–47, 51).

Rowland and Frank examine Greater Israel ideology and Palestinian Islamic fundamentalist discourse side by side to reveal the similar rhetorical features that constitute the oppositional narrative frames. They contend that Greater Israel and Palestinian Islamic fundamentalist extreme narratives are entelechial, which explains both sides' willingness to use violence in order to achieve the end of mythic perfection. Drawing from Burke, Rowland and Frank define entelechy as a "symbolic force that causes humans to extend an idea to the 'end of the line' in search of perfection, which often produces terrible results" ("Mythic" 43). According to their study, Palestinian and Israeli entelechial narratives share rhetorical moves such as the villain-hero-victim drama triangle, mythic claims to sacred land, the complete negation of the other's identity, and the linkage of modern-day struggle to a heroic past of righteous ancestors. Although both extreme narratives frame the other as its evil enemy and victimizer, an additional rhetorical move they share is what they frame as the ultimate cause of their own suffering. For Begin, ultimate responsibility for the Holocaust was Jewish weakness and passivity. For Hamas, "the ultimate cause of the Palestinian exile is that Palestinians have turned away from Islam" (Rowland and Frank, "Mythic" 51). As a call to arms, Zionist military force can redeem itself of the Holocaust; Palestinians have lost their way from Islam but can return through the path of Jihad.

Amidst the historical narrative of Jewish suffering, uptake triggers within the Israeli frame position Palestinian terrorists as the embodied thousands-years-old anti-Jewish persecutor. The trauma from the past gets taken up in the present to make sense of the current reality, and Palestinian resistance is registered as an atomized antisemitic attack. In other words, the only possible motivation for Hamas' attacks, for instance, is discriminatory hatred of the Jews, as though there is no other plausible motive or reason. Abraham deliberates the controversial equation of anti-Israel politics with anti-Jewish hatred, or that anti-Zionism is the new antisemitism.[40] He writes, "Hamas can be compared to the Nazis because as an organization it is dedicated to the destruction of Israel as a Jewish state; however, one cannot simply state that Hamas is driven to destroy Israel because of anti-Semitism. Instead, one must recognize that Hamas seeks Israel's destruction because Israel is viewed as occupying and colonizing Palestinian land" ("Reluctant Rhetoricians" 46). Hamas, a Palestinian Sunni-Islamist fundamentalist organization with social services and military wings, was founded in 1987 when the First Intifada began. Founded more than twenty years earlier in 1964, the secular nationalist Palestine Liberation Organization (PLO) also took up armed struggle as a resistance strategy.

Situated in the larger context of anticolonial Third World internationalist movements from the 1950s through the eighties, Said argues that the "principle of 'armed struggle' derives from the right of resistance accorded universally to all peoples suffering national oppression" ("The Essential" 153). In basic terms, then, the dominant Palestinian narrative frame of armed struggle sees their use of force as a legitimate right, which in its mirror image the Israeli frame rejects as terrorism. On a fundamental level, Israel's rationale for violence has the law of the

---

[40] For example, see texts such as Rosenfeld, ed., *Anti-Zionism and Antisemitism: The Dynamics of Deligitimization*, and Nelson, *Israel Denial: Anti-Zionism, Anti-Semitism, and the Faculty Campaign Against the Jewish State* for cases that argue anti-Zionist politics equates to the new antisemitism.

state behind it, and Palestinian armed struggle does not. Chomsky argues, "In the view of the

apologist for state terror, resistance to an occupying army or its local mercenaries is terrorism,

meriting harsh reprisal" ("Middle East" 107). The Palestinian struggle for sovereignty can be

characterized by three overall strategies: negotiations and international diplomacy, nonviolent

unarmed resistance and civil disobedience, and armed struggle. With regard to diplomacy and

negotiations, for instance, in 1976 the PLO and Arab states submitted a two-state peace proposal

to the United Nations, which Israel rejected (Elgindy 94–99).[41]

Political scientist Dov Waxman calls the decade from 1967–1977 a period of "devotion"

between American Jews and the State of Israel that unapologetically supported Israel "right or

wrong." He writes, "The widespread fear of a second Holocaust prior to the [1967] war, followed

by the relief and jubilation felt after Israel's swift and stunning victory, led to a spontaneous

outpouring of support for Israel from American Jews" (35). Post-WWII and prior to the 1961

Eichmann trial and 1967 Six-Day War, Novick argues that Israel and the Holocaust were not

central issues on American Jewish minds nor their identity like they became afterward (121,

144).[42] Through the 1970s, events such as the 1972 Munich massacre, the 1973 October War,

and the 1975 UN Resolution 3379 in effect confirmed the State of Israel's sense of

"vulnerability, of its isolated and beleaguered situation" in conjunction with the American and

Israeli shared frame's preconceived notion that political criticism and armed attack against Israel

was antisemitic in nature (Novick 160). Whereas the U.S. and Israel deemed the PLO a terrorist

---

[41] In addition to Elgindy, *Blind Spot: America and the Palestinians, from Balfour to Trump*, see also Anziska, *Preventing Palestine: A Political History from Camp David to Oslo* and Chomsky, *Fateful Triangle: The United States, Israel, and the Palestinians* for details of the ways in which Israel refused to negotiate with the Palestinian national movement in the 1970s. Said poignantly states, "In fact, Israel will not negotiate with nor recognize the PLO precisely because it does represent the Palestinians" (*The Question* xix).

[42] Novick contends, "The Eichmann trial, along with the controversies over Arendt's book and Hochhuth's play, effectively broke fifteen years of near silence on the Holocaust in American public discourse. As part of this process, there emerged in American culture a distinct *thing* called 'the Holocaust'—an event in its own right, not simply a subdivision of general Nazi barbarism" (144, *original emphasis*).

organization, elsewhere the PLO was gaining international legitimacy as a representative body of the Palestinian people.[43] The United Nations granted the PLO observer status in the 1974 Resolution 3237, and one year later the UN adopted Resolution 3379 that determined Zionism is a "form of racism and racial discrimination." From a Holocaust-centered worldview, such events lead to the logical conclusion that political criticism of Zionism equates to anti-Jewish animus against Israel.

Waxman argues that following the 1967–1977 period of devotion transpired a period of disillusionment, which has lingered to present day. He asks the question, "Why have growing numbers of American Jews become disenchanted with Israel and more critical of it since the late 1970s?" (*Trouble* 41) and identifies three overall turning points: the Likud party win in 1977, Israel's 1979 peace treaty with Egypt, and increasing American Jewish engagement with and knowledge about Israel, which, Waxman argues, essentially began and continues to disrupt idyllic fantasies of the State of Israel with harsh on-the-ground realities.

The policies of Menachem Begin and Likud party proved a stark and upsetting contrast to many American Jews' idealized picture of Israel. Begin had "promised that, if elected, he would never return the territories Israel had occupied in the June 1967 war" (Pappé, *The Biggest* 154). Thus, such diverging views from liberal democracy toward ethno-nationalist supremacy were especially evident in Begin's territorial maximalism and support of Israeli Jewish settlements in the occupied territories, in addition to his hawkish outlook and conduct in the 1982 Lebanon War. Although many liberal American Jews believed in and romanticized Israel as a peace-seeking social democracy that fought just wars with a morally pure army, historian Ilan Pappé argues against a false dichotomy that idealizes a pre-1967 and pre-Likud egalitarian Israeli

---

[43] See Said, *The Question of Palestine*, pp. xviii, 157–169.

culture. He writes, "The impulse for taking over the West Bank and the Gaza Strip is the same that led the Zionist leadership to ethnically cleanse much of Palestine in 1948 and to other policies of oppression and dispossession implemented against the Palestinians wherever they were" (155).

At the same time that there was more outspoken criticism into the 1980s, the majority of American Jews still held tightly to the mythic image of Israel as "David versus Goliath" and remained rather ignorant about and even uninterested in the history of the Arab-Israeli conflict and the nature of Zionist ideology and Israeli politics. Waxman contends, "Since Israel was primarily a symbol of Jewishness to American Jews, their support for Israel was fundamentally an expression of support for Jewishness and for the Jewish people. As such, Israel's actual behavior and policies were of no great concern to American Jews" (*Trouble* 47). The second turning point listed above is significant in terms of Holocaust associations with pro-Israel rhetoric in binary opposition to Arab and Islamic terrorism. Waxman zooms out from intracommunal Israeli politics to the larger Arab-Israeli conflict and points to Israel's 1979 peace treaty with Egypt as a turning point in perceptions of Jewish power, which saw the shift from interstate warfare between Israel and Arab countries to asymmetrical warfare between the IDF and nonstate actors operating in densely populated civilian areas. He argues, "It was no longer David against the Arab Goliath; instead, in a role reversal, Israel became Goliath and the Palestinians became David—widely perceived as the weaker, more vulnerable party in the conflict" (*Trouble* 45).

Regardless, then-PM of Israel Menachem Begin saw the PLO as a neo-Nazi terrorist organization and based on this belief refused to sit at the negotiating table with them as political representatives of the Palestinian people and nationalist cause. Instead, he saw any and all Israeli use of force and brutality against Palestinian resistance as entirely legitimate in the name of

Jewish security and Israel's right to defend itself as a sovereign nation. The burst in previous

perception from devotion to disillusionment came to an even greater turning point with Israel's

invasion of Lebanon in June 1982 and the resulting Sabra and Shatila massacre that the IDF

facilitated to the horror of many. Novick argues, "Inflicting mass devastation on the civilian

population of Beirut was, in Begin's view, justified, because 1982 was just like 1945: Arafat in

Beirut was Hitler in his bunker under the Reichschancellery" (161).

Through decontextualization and a Holocaust-centered worldview, Zionism's Third

Persona enables a view from afar in the American Jewish community of Israel as a morally pure

and just nation that can do no wrong. For instance, Chomsky details the 1985 events of

Operation Wooden Leg, an Israeli attack on the PLO headquarters in Tunisia killing civilian

noncombatants including children. He exposes the U.S.-Israeli use of pretext, charges of Arab

rejectionism, and the concept of retaliation as strategies that not only work to silence dissent and

cover over U.S.-Israeli abuse of power, but also to invert the position of offense as one of

defense. Embedded in this inversion is the underlying logic that *they* are terrorists, and *we* are

not. Chomsky argues, "These crucial political realities provide the necessary framework for any

discussion of 'the evil scourge of terrorism,' which, in the racist terms of American discourse,

refers to terrorist acts by Arabs, but not by Jews, just as 'peace' means a settlement that honors

the right of national self-determination of Jews, but not of Palestinians" ("Middle East" 99).

Further effacing any semblance of human-ness, rhetorical strategies such as pretext and

retaliation objectify *them* as pathologically deviant terrorists and render *us* as acting justly in the

name of self-defense.

Said elaborates on this objectification of the Arab Other in his critical review of the 1987

anthology *Terrorism: How the West Can Win* edited by Benjamin Netanyahu, then-Ambassador

to the United Nations and later Prime Minister of Israel from 1996–1999, and 2009 to present (as

of this writing). In *Terrorism*, Netanyahu writes: "The root cause of terrorism lies not in

grievances but in a disposition toward unbridled violence. This can be traced to a world view

which asserts that certain ideological and religious goals justify, indeed demand, the shedding of

all moral inhibitions. In this context, the observation that the root cause of terrorism is terrorists

is more than a tautology" (qtd. in Said, "The Essential" 154). In their respective essays both

Chomsky and Said show how, in the larger context of the Cold War, the dominant U.S.-Israeli

shared frame render democracy and freedom as under attack by the barbaric nonwhite Other that

at once embodies the threat of communism and terrorism. As the quote by Netanyahu reveals,

the embodiment of existential threat is seen as a form of inherent barbarism with "a disposition

toward unbridled violence." According to this worldview, Israelis have no choice but to retaliate

as such.

In his review, Said argues that the anthology's authors neglect historical perspective and

omit cultural context, thereby enabling a colonialist and racist view of the Arab Other as an

inherently evil terrorist. Said is by no means condoning attacks on Israeli civilian casualties and

criticizes the PLO for misdirected over-emphasis on armed struggle. He writes, "But the

tragically fixated attitude toward 'armed struggle' conducted from exile and the relative neglect

of mass political action and organization inside Palestine exposed the Palestinian movement, by

the early 1970s, to a far superior Israeli military and propaganda system, which magnified

Palestinian violence out of proportion to the reality" ("The Essential" 153). Said shows that

studies such as Netanyahu's *Terrorism* carry an authoritative weight that works to confirm previously held biases by policymakers, diplomats, lobbyists, and other high-ranking officials.

The discourse on terrorism produces a knowable, containable enemy for an otherwise historical

Palestinian movement with legitimate political demands for self-determination in their native

homeland. Israeli security rhetoric relies upon dehumanizing language of the Arab Other, figured

in tropes of irrationality, religious fanaticism, and overreaction, in order to justify its protocol of

brute force retaliation.[44]

Rhetorical Dissociation in Hertzberg's Open Letter

In the opening to his 1999 book *The Holocaust in American Life*, Novick reflects on what

led him to spend years researching the topic. He says that, as a historian, he was curious as to

why, "in 1990s America—fifty years after the fact and thousands of miles from its site—the

Holocaust [had] come to loom so large in our culture." As an American and a Jew, Novick says

he felt skeptical as to whether such a development is as desirable as "most people seem to think

---

[44] Israel uses military force to protect Jewish settlements in the West Bank. In order to build more Jewish settlements, Israel expropriates Palestinians' farmland and grazing areas and appropriates water sources, all of which prevents Palestinian access to their livelihood and previously relied upon water sources ("Settlements").

For example, the Halamish settlement has been implicated in ongoing disputes with the nearby residents of Nabi Salih, who argue that Israeli Halamish settlers began taking over the water spring in 2009, on top of which blocks the Nabi Salih residents from working their farmlands around the spring. For three years, Nabi Salih's residents held weekly demonstrations to protest the takeover. Amira Hass documented Nabi Saleh's popular uprising. She writes, "Huge quantities of tear gas, rubber-coated bullets flying between buildings, gas canisters with (illegally) extended ranges, beatings, shovings and home invasions—this is what the Israel Defense Forces employs against the small village of 500" ("Mighty Israel"). Upon initial labor preparing for the construction of the Halamish settlement in the late 1970s, the other nearby village, Dir Nizam, claimed ownership of Havlata Hill, which was denied through Israel's use of the Ottoman Land Code. Havlata Hill is now the center of the Halamish settlement. Later on, in Nabi Saleh, "[s]ince the demonstrations began in 2009, 155 of the residents have been injured, forty percent of whom are children. Thirty-five houses have been damaged in the process of dispersing demonstrations, and seven caught fire" (Hass). Today Halamish continues to expand and build houses on land belonging to the villages of Nabi Saleh and Dir Nizam, where punitive demolitions also continue when Palestinians build homes without Israeli permits to do so. See footnote 29.

Nabi Saleh's popular uprising is a case of nonviolent resistance and civil disobedience whereby Israel reacts with brute force: Palestinian protestors shouting and throwing stones against IDF soldiers firing tear gas canisters and rubber-coated bullets. Tear gas is a chemical weapon that causes severe eye, respiratory, and skin irritation, pain, bleeding, and even blindness. The IDF uses tear gas canisters with extended ranges, which are illegal (Hass). Rubber bullets are intended to be a non-lethal alternative to metal bullets, causing bruises, abrasions, and broken bones, but can still result in death.

it is" (1). The conclusions of his book proved controversial. Not a history about the Holocaust

itself, but a historiography about how the Holocaust is discussed, deployed, memorialized, and

depicted in America, Novick determines, "For many Jews, though this is much less true than it

was a few years ago, it has mandated an intransigent and self-righteous posture in the Israeli-

Palestinian conflict. … And in this realm the Holocaust framework has promoted as well a

belligerent stance toward any criticism of Israel" (10). In this sense, he argues, the domineering

lesson of the Holocaust in American life, and in Israel, is one of ominous anti-Jewish animus

lurking just below the surface. Novick concludes, "The identical talk of uniqueness and

incomparability surrounding the Holocaust in the United States performs the opposite function: it

promotes *evasion* of moral and historical responsibility" (15, *original emphasis*).

Fig. 1. Front cover to the August 1988 issue of *The New York Review of Books* featuring Hertzberg's open letter;

"Table of Contents; August 18, 1988"; nybooks.com, https://www.nybooks.com/issues/1988/08/18/.

In this section, I look at Wiesel's *New York Times* editorial "A Mideast Peace – Is It

Impossible?" published June 1988, and Hertzberg's critical response in the form of an open letter published two months later in *The New York Review of Books* (see fig. 1). Rhetorically, open letters have been used as a strategy to expose hegemonic logics that justify the status quo of oppression. From Émile Zola's 1898 open letter "J'Accuse…!" that accuses the French government of antisemitism during the Dreyfus affair, to Dr. Martin Luther King, Jr.'s 1963 "Letter from Birmingham Jail" that refutes the claims of white moderates to wait for justice to come through the courts, to Hertzberg's "An Open Letter to Elie Wiesel" that appeals to the Jewish tradition of advocating on behalf of the stranger to support Palestinian rights, open letters have been a way to call attention to injustice. Whereas Wiesel expresses concern that criticism of Israel inflames animus toward the state,[45] for Hertzberg, it is because of Jewish morality that he opposes the military crackdown on Palestinian protesters. The epistolary form of the open letter enables Hertzberg to communicate a deeply personal and felt message that reflects his sense of self in direct relation to the forensic discourse of the larger issue. As such, the open letter is compelling in its ability to simultaneously address two different audiences: the addressee's doxastic audience, and the reinvented audience who will more readily accept a daring break with protocol.

In his editorial, Wiesel presents what he believes to be a moderate political position with regard to Israeli security but which Hertzberg critiques as "an elegant defense of the Likud [right-wing] hard line." Published in 1988 after the start of the First Palestinian Intifada, Wiesel justifies Israeli military force by exceptionalizing Jewish suffering as distinct from (yet constituted through the disavowal of) the Palestinian Other. For Wiesel, therein lies a conflict of

---

[45] Within the dominant American and Israeli shared frame, outspoken Jewish criticism of Israel and anti-occupation dissent is cast as harmful to Jewish unity. In a 1988 news report "Israeli Policies Split U.S. Jewish Opinion" from the *Chicago Tribune*, journalists McNulty et al. inquire into "the proper role of American Jews in Israeli policy" and argue, "A strong current running under the debate is the fear that criticism will erode support for Israel. Some Jews also fear that criticism of the Jewish state may translate into criticism of Jews and feed anti-Semitism."

moral principles with the need for security. On the one hand, he declares, "Self-determination is a sacred principle of civilized society," and on the other, he asks, "Isn't a Jew called upon to be sensitive to his fellow human beings' concerns? How then is one to reconcile the needs of security with Judaism's concept of humanism?" Hertzberg's letter offers an answer to Wiesel's contradiction in principles with a critique based in Jewish tradition and Holocaust memory. In his letter, Hertzberg asks Wiesel: "What have we learned from the murder of our families? How must we live with their memory? You and I read and reread the Bible and Talmud: What do the sacred texts command us to think, to feel, and to do?" The letter offers a Jewish rhetoric of identity that departs from dominant discourse and reinvents collective self-understanding in relation to Palestinian rights, not uniquely separate from.

Wiesel opens his editorial in Gaza, pondering the circumstances. He informally interviews Palestinian lawyer Fayez Abu Rahme and asks questions about the Israeli military. About Rahme's aspirations, Wiesel quotes him saying, "A Palestinian state. Demilitarized. The police would carry sticks, not guns." Then, Wiesel poses a question to his doxastic reader: "Did he [Rahme] understand Israel's permanent fears for its security?" The editorial proceeds from informal dialogue with Rahme to a scene with Israeli soldiers; Wiesel remarks on how young they are, and do they know Palestinians want freedom and a future? How should they respond to Palestinian suffering? He quotes Israel Defense Forces (IDF) soldiers who say, "What do they want us to do? Uprising means war. We have no choice but to defend ourselves" and "It is not our fault that the enemy hides behind children."

Wiesel situates himself as a reasonable, middle ground observer by juxtaposing the two conversations, from Palestinian to Israeli. He contends that he sympathizes with the frustration and anger on both sides, the Palestinians who are "treated as nonpersons" and the Israeli soldiers who are wrongly depicted as "sadists." Wiesel discusses what he argues are negative images of Israel in the media that portray IDF soldiers as "bloodthirsty," with some extreme cases in "pro-Arab circles" of Israel "being compared to Hitler's Germany, its policy to Nazism and the Palestinians of today to the Jews of yesterday." He asks, "How are we to convince Israel's political adversaries that the Holocaust is beyond politics and beyond analogies?"

By contending that the Holocaust is "beyond politics and analogies," Wiesel positions the Holocaust in terms of ahistorical myth. It is through this mythos that Wiesel reconciles the subjugation of Palestinians in the name of self-defense with the principle of self-determination. Novick argues, "As the Holocaust moved from history to myth, it became the bearer of 'eternal truths' not bound by historical circumstances. … With this mindset, there could be no such thing as overreaction to an anti-Semitic incident, no such thing as exaggerating the omnipresent danger" (178). Wiesel is at a loss for where to turn and how to resolve the Israeli-Palestinian conflict, on the premise that, "As long as the P.L.O. remains a terrorist organization, as long as it has not given up on its goal of destroying Israel, why should Israel negotiate with its leaders? But then, if the P.L.O. is not an interlocutor, who could be?" To Wiesel, even though Israel wants peace, they have no negotiating partner. Even though Israel wants peace, they have no choice but to defend themselves. Although Israel is the dominant military force in an asymmetrical power relationship to stateless Palestinians, Wiesel suggests that Israel is the one victimized by Arab terrorism and is doing its moral best despite the constraints. He argues, "Israel is the only country that feels its existence threatened."

In historical context, Wiesel was wary of outspoken criticism of the occupation in fear of "splitting the Jewish community" and posing a "risk" to Israel (qtd. in Hertzberg). Within the dominant Zionist frame, Jewish criticism of Israel is stigmatized as harmful to Jewish unity.

Hertzberg writes, "The most effective device of these hard-liners has been to suggest that *any* criticism of their position is a self-hating assault on the state when such criticism is uttered by Jews, and that it is a form of anti-Semitism when it is spoken by non-Jews" (*original emphasis*). Although Wiesel spoke out against apartheid South Africa, Bosnian genocide, and the crisis in Darfur, among many other causes, when it came to supporting Israel, he ascribed to a belief of omnipresent antisemitic danger embodied by the Arab Islamic terrorist. In the open letter, Hertzberg confronts Wiesel's contradiction in principles: "In the memory of the Holocaust we have been reminded by you that silence is a sin. You have spoken out against indifference and injustice. Why are you making a special exception of Israel? Do you think that our silence will help Israel?" Hertzberg reframes Holocaust memory in alignment with the moral principle of speaking out against injustice, instead of drawing upon Holocaust memory to exceptionalize Jewish suffering as "beyond politics" to rationalize the cognitive dissonance.

In the 1980s, conditions for Palestinians living under military occupation only worsened. Israel continued to dispossess Palestinians from their land and Jewish settlers intimidated Palestinians with vigilante attacks, placing bombs in cars and setting fire to Palestinian farmland (all of which continues today). Throughout the First Intifada, the IDF imposed strict curfews, conducted mass arrests, and inflicted collective punishment with checkpoints and mobility restrictions and by closing schools and businesses. Then-Defense Minister Yitzhak Rabin implemented the infamous "broken bones" policy, ordering IDF soldiers to break the limbs of Palestinian demonstrators. In the U.S. and around the world, viewers were shocked by news footage of Israeli military suppression of Palestinian popular protest.

In his open letter, Hertzberg uses dissociative strategies to expose an incompatibility of perception with reality. Rhetorical dissociation entails renaming a situation when the audience has other terms in mind. Authors and speakers can use dissociation as a way to distinguish inconsistency and make an appeal to see the situation at hand in a different way. By appealing to Wiesel's doxastic audience, Hertzberg offers a "forceful presentation of the incompatibility" to which the reinvented audience accepts (Perelman and Olbrechts-Tyteca 413). Although Hertzberg disagrees with Wiesel and seeks to reveal the limits of his reasoning and reframe belief, Hertzberg nonetheless shares common ground and identifies with him. According to Kenneth Burke's theory of rhetoric as identification, common ground can both contain consubstantiality and enable the transposition of its terms.[46] Through the reconstitution of his Jewish self-understanding that de-stigmatizes speaking out, Hertzberg redraws discursive boundaries and creates space for dissident voices to become legible within the larger community.

Hertzberg recalls Wiesel's belief that "'self-determination is a sacred principle,' one that [Wiesel] believe[s] should apply to the Palestinians." Based on this sacred principle, Hertzberg contends, dissent becomes a moral directive when such principles are violated. Wiesel fails to do this and in effect forgoes his own principles in the name of Israeli security and Jewish unity. Hertzberg evokes the tradition of Hebrew prophets who voice opposition to the prophets of the royal courts. He argues, "The biblical prophets were harassed as traitors who weakened the resolve of a small people—but it is their 'treason,' and not the prudence of the court prophets, that is our unique Jewish tradition." Hertzberg reminds Wiesel of Nathan, "who dared to confront King David with murdering Uriah and stealing his wife. Nathan defended this Hittite stranger against a divinely appointed Jewish king: 'You are the man,' he said to David: you are morally responsible." Whereas Wiesel constitutes Jewish fidelity in terms of unquestioned

---

[46] While consubstantiality means A identifies with B, or that A and B share common ground, Burke contends it is also common ground that "makes for transformability. At every point where the field covered by any one of these terms overlaps upon the field covered by any other, there is an alchemic opportunity" (*A Grammar* xix). See chapter three for further examination of this concept.

loyalty to the State of Israel, Hertzberg draws upon tradition and reconstitutes Jewishness as a moral mandate to advocate on behalf of the stranger in an ethical relation to alterity.

Put differently, Hertzberg transposes the terms of unquestioned pro-Israel support into an ethical relation that sees self-determination for the stranger as bound up with the unforeseeable fate of one's own. The form of the open letter enables an address to a specific individual and by extension the addressee's doxastic audience, in addition to the reinvented audience akin to Hertzberg's readership that more readily accepts his daring break with protocol. Philosophers Chaïm Perelman and Lucie Olbrechts-Tyteca argue, "It can be said that audiences pass judgment on one another" (35). In this rhetorical setup, Hertzberg invites Wiesel's audience to identify with Hertzberg's through a dissociation of procedure, where he offers a "forceful presentation of the incompatibility" that reveals the limits of Wiesel's reasoning. That is to say, the reinvented audience is invited to pass judgment on the previously incarnated doxastic audience as a way to validate the reframed concept (Schilb 39). Perelman and Olbrechts-Tyteca write, "The dissociation of concepts ... involves a more profound change that is always prompted by the desire to remove an incompatibility arising out of the confrontation of one proposition with others, whether one is dealing with norms, facts, or truths" (413). Hertzberg's letter exhibits a dissociation of concepts that implicates a profound change in Jewish identity in relation to Israel by reframing the Zionist mythos of *meSho'ah le-tekumah* (from Holocaust to rebirth).

Coming to terms with the sacred principle of self-determination for Palestinians and dissent as moral responsibility challenges the fundamental logic underlying what Hertzberg refers to as the "Likud hardline," or Greater Israel ideology that excludes non-Jews. It is not only that the dominant Zionist narrative negates Palestinian identity, but also that this negation makes possible the extension and affirmation of Zionist mythic identity to the end of the line. Thus, to expose the contradictory logic of this narrative is to call into question the essential substance of Jewish ethnonational identity. Hertzberg dissociates from Wiesel's connecting links and turns the threat on its head by recasting the Palestinian Other from antisemitic terrorist into the stranger that Hebrew prophets stand up for. The real threat, Hertzberg suggests, is the failure to extend the principle of self-determination to others.

Chapter 3

Interrupting Identity, or Heeding the Call for Justice

As I have illustrated thus far in chapters one and two, the contemporary Jewish rhetoric of dissent regarding the State of Israel and Palestinian rights has emerged from the 125-year-old tradition of dissent since Zionism took root in the late nineteenth century. While the dissenting binational rhetoric of Jewish-Arab cooperation has been silenced throughout this era, in the past fifteen years, there has been a shift in the American public discourse that legitimizes dissent.

This chapter is concerned with the ways that the contemporary rhetoric of dissent redraws the contours of Jewish identity in an ethical relationship with the Palestinian Other through the rhetorical strategy of first-person identity reconstitution. Dissenters reinvent Jewish identity through self-reflection on scenes of interruption that transform their sense of who they are in relation to Palestinian suffering. In what follows, I explore the rhetoric of first-person narratives of identity reconstitution as a form of political dissent. I argue for the formulation of a rhetorical framework that understands identity as an everyday practice and may potentially progress toward developing an ethical relationship with alterity (i.e., otherness, abjection, or the state of being foreign).

As I discussed in chapters one and two, Zionism advocates for Jewish national self-determination and the right to exist as a state. Over the past fifty to seventy-five years, being pro-Israel or a Zionist has become enmeshed in memories of the Holocaust and what it means to be Jewish in the United States. I am interested in the rhetorical construction of dominant narratives concerning Israel's right to exist and defend itself, as well as the ways that these discourses frame Palestinians' struggle for freedom. Under a dominant Zionist framework, Palestinian self-representation is disregarded and denied. Furthermore, as I established in chapters one and two,

representations *about* Palestinians through the shared U.S.-Israeli lens tend to objectify them into

four categories: (1) antisemitic terrorists, (2) rejectionists of peace offers, (3) corrupt and unable

to self-govern, as well as (4) self-inflicted victims. By utilizing two case studies of textual

artifacts by critics Sara Roy and Peter Beinart, I delineate a countertradition of Jewish dissent

that builds upon the discursive intervention of Hertzberg's open letter and recuperates the

Palestinians as partners of the dialogue. I demonstrate that not only are the dissenters speaking

out in support of Palestinian rights, but they are also asserting what their Jewish identity means

to them.

Identity as Rhetorical Strategy

In response to Palestinian suffering and their calls for justice, a common theme of

dissenters' narratives concerns how their Jewish identities have been shattered or deeply

challenged, which has initiated the reinvention of their identity in relation to Palestinian rights.

First, I examine this interruption and self-reconstitution of identity in Peter Beinart's 2012 book,

The Crisis of Zionism, and then, I discuss it through the lens of Sara Roy's 2002 lecture and

essay, "Living with the Holocaust: The Journey of a Child of Holocaust Survivors."

The rhetorical analysis of first-person identity narratives focuses on how the author

strategically fashions a story to address certain occasions and purposes as well as in response to a

situation where the author's identity is constituted. In this sense, the self's identity is a rhetorical

situation that narrates personal realities through stories, which authors and speakers share about

themselves to an audience in order to compose a sense of self-understanding. Compositionist

Candace Spigelman writes, "I want to emphasize that although writers may organize their stories of experience into single sentences or as lengthy chronological accounts, in the kind of personal writing I have in mind, the telling is *purposeful* and intended to do more than express an opinion or cathartically confess" (6, *original emphasis*). Spigelman argues in a similar vein to Anderson regarding the rhetorical aspect of first-person narrative, that it can function less as a mode of emotive self-divulgence (as it is sometimes viewed) and more as strategic self-reflection and appropriate disclosure, as a way of making an argument. According to Anderson, these stories become "self-constituted acts by which individuals articulate their identities in discourse" (38). Identity is understood not as a metaphysical self that can transcend material-symbolic context, but as a rhetorical strategy that seeks to compose self-understanding through the interlocutors of the stories. Thus, first-person identity constitution is concerned with how the rhetoric of identity narrates the self-understanding of personal realities to an audience, which Anderson terms, "expressible self-interpretation" (11).

Within this theoretical framework, identification and identity are context-specific, unending processes of negotiation. Identity narratives are simultaneously reified and engrained, while also being open to change as each rhetorical situation unfolds. According to Burke's dictum, "To identify A with B is to make A 'consubstantial' with B" (*A Rhetoric* 21), so A may identify with B, but it is not identical. Burke argues that no two things, people, or situations are exactly the same. Burke postulates that there is an inherent ambiguity in the nature of language, but instead of being a problem to solve, it can be utilized as a resource (Anderson 24). In fact, it is an infinite resource, as Burke says, "it is in the areas of ambiguity that transformation takes place" (*A Grammar* xix). Therefore, consubstantiality means that A and B share a commonality, which means that they symbolically relate in their identification to one another. Rhetorician Ann E. Berthoff refers to this phenomenon as the hypostatic power of language whereby substance solidifies into discernible matter and definable terms amidst the ongoing dialectic of meaning-making, communication, and interpretation.

The Greek word, *hypostasis*, describes an essential, stable foundation that supports everything in existence, like a glue that holds the universe together in a state of chaotic orderliness. For example, in medical science, hypostasis is used to describe the settling of blood that occurs in dependent organs and parts of the body under the influence of gravity. Geologically, hypostasis can also be understood as sedimentary phenomena, like the ways that organic particles settle or fall into place; it is simultaneously a deliberate occurrence and happenstance. Berthoff presents language as a hypostatic power of the *animal symbolicum* (i.e., the human as a meaning-making creature), which privileges language as an essential component to humanity's existence. She argues that all knowledge is partial and a human's capacity for knowledge is an innate "God-given power" (750). In this sense, then, consubstantiality means A and B share commonality, a congealing ground upon which A and B symbolically relate in identification with one another. Rhetorician Krista Ratcliffe contends, "Burke's identification makes space for personal agency and commonalities but not for differences" (58). Ratcliffe argues that Burke's theory of rhetoric as identification relies upon a sense of common ground that in turn effaces difference. Here, I am interested in moments of identification that in effect interrupt a coherent sense of self or insular identity, whereby the interruption does not dismiss difference or enforce some kind of commonality but rather engenders a self-reflective awareness in relation to alterity that can be mobilized into a regular ethical practice.

In other words, I explore the disruption of identity's sedimentation in the rhetoric of first-person identity reconstitution that illustrates the process whereby preconceived belief systems are challenged and demands from the foreign Other become audible to the self. In the dissenters' narratives exhibited in this chapter, the demand of alterity becomes audible through nonlinear processes of attunement, such as moral shock or jolting encounters alongside gradual awareness and self-reflection. Philosopher Bruno Latour contends, "The first time you hear it, any fresh revival of an old theme will necessarily sound shrill, intolerable, inaudible, cacophonous. You have first to get the ear used to the new sound, to the revival in a new key of the exact same old tune" (10). In this way, I argue for rhetorical attunement in the kairotic moments of identification that *interrupt* (rather than reinstate) a coherent sense of self, just as a traditional tune can be recalibrated to render a new sound of ethical relationality.

At first glance, poststructuralist and postmodern criticism may suggest that this framework caters to an overly individualistic sense of self that neglects socially constructed aspects of selfhood and unwittingly perpetuates an essentialist perspective of identity politics. For instance, historian Joan Scott argues that studying first-person narratives can preclude consideration for how personal identity categories became possible in the first place. Scott contends, "Making visible the experience of a different group exposes the existence of repressive mechanisms, but not their inner workings or logics" (779). Relying on knowable experiences reinstates the underlying assumptions of identity and naturalizes its terms; therefore, questions are ignored concerning how experience is socially mediated or how subjects are produced through discourse.

To critically engage with the terms of our inquiries, according to Scott, we must historicize them, which entails understanding "all categories of analysis as contextual, contested, and contingent" and considering "the effects of their articulations" (796). Historicization can become a means of destabilizing the notion of identity as insular and fixed. Scott illustrates this point in her rereading of a scene in Samuel Delany's autobiography, *The Motion of Light in*

Water, which is about his first visit to the St. Mark's bathhouse in 1963. Delany "remembers standing on the threshold of a 'gym-sized room' dimly lit by blue bulbs." The room was full of bodies and the sight, for Delany, gives him a "sense of participation in a movement" (774). Scott starts her essay with the type of reading that she would prefer to avoid regarding visibility politics that claims to render voice to the voiceless as a correction to the oversights of dominant discourse but fails to question the mechanisms of injustice. She argues that this form of visibility politics ends up essentializing identity, while the terms that are used to correct the oversights utilize the same logic that first creates alterity and oppression. Scott seeks to defamiliarize and undo the terms to decenter hegemonic power and reframe the possible approaches to understand these structures.

In her second reading of Delany, Scott illustrates how a "dim blue light" can be read as a medium through which experience is projected and represented. This describes a moment that calls attention to the constructed, fragmented, and fraught nature of subject formation and the ways *identity* and *community* are constituted through discourse and historical memory. Thus, the bathhouse example becomes a scene of identification, relations, and a question of representation, rather than providing empirical proof that one *is* authentically gay in some "prediscursive reality" or that gay communities have any essential foundation that may become dangerous or pathologically deviant (794). While Scott does not seek to reify the terms of legitimized violence and discrimination, he does question the representation of experience to expose new frameworks of thought regarding the logic of human existence.

The rhetoric of first-person identity constitution does not take for granted the terms of an author's represented personal reality or the evidence of their experience. This self-understanding is constituted through discourse to reflect both its dialectical and paradoxical nature. Rhetorical iterations, such as utterances, inscriptions, and images enable meaning, which is made possible when drawn from preexisting intertextual and asymmetrical relations or discursive matrices of power/knowledge relations. Scott argues, "It is not individuals who have experience, but subjects who are constituted through experience" (779), but I think individuals have experience and are also constituted through those experiences. The individual and the experience differentially influence each other, so the problem of identity becomes a "perpetual interplay between the individual and the world by which both shape, and reshape, their senses of who they are" (Anderson 32–33). Moreover, while first-person identity constitution does presume an author or speaker's agency, I agree with Anderson's idea that it is not over-determined or a type of metaphysical essence that exists prior to discourse. Anderson contends that Burke challenges the traditional principle of rhetoric as persuasion (i.e., his theory of rhetoric as identification) because it "presupposes a conscious awareness in both speaker and audience that would occlude the many unconscious ways in which people are moved toward belief and action" (25).

Anderson argues for an approach to identity "as a function of the terms that 'conspire' and 'mutually adjust' to 'round out' a characterization of its 'substance', an effect of the 'equations it inevitably embodies in its action as an evolving unity'" (31). In other words, the terms that enact identity compose its constitutive substance and work as boundary markers that simultaneously enable and constrain it to become comprehensible within "what the pentad describes as a 'scene-act ratio'" (43). In a given scene, which is examined through what Anderson refers to as, the "'circumferential logic' of interpretation," there "are different *circumferences* that one must draw around an act in order to interpret it, encircling it in contexts as broad or as narrow as one chooses, containing it within a range of possibilities that this circumference inscribes" (44). In this way, a constitution "substantiates a particular scene in which certain motives are possible" (Anderson 48). In the following section, I examine scenes of

interruption, which Burke refers to as alchemic opportunities for transformation, whereby the

terms that once conspired to fulfill the identification of A with B are called into question and

transposed. In the two different first-person dissenting narratives, I look at the ways that the

authors' self-defined ideals and motivations become embroiled in an agonistic struggle of

identity in a scene of interruption. I argue that the dissenters employ traditional Jewish tunes to

understand the recent realities of Israel's abuse of power in their advocacy for Palestinian human

rights.

The Interruption and Reinvention of Identity

The Crisis of Zionism by Peter Beinart is not an autobiography but an editorial account

that reviews the past several decades to reflect on the relationship between the American Jewish

establishment and State of Israel to ponder how they have arrived at what Beinart see as the

current state of crisis. Beinart demonstrates how this is not only a political crisis between Israelis

and Palestinians, but it is also an identity crisis for American Jews. *The Crisis of Zionism*

presents journalistic research and political argument as a call to action, and Beinart significantly

utilizes the first-person narrative to begin his book by discussing his family history, including an

intimate portrayal of his grandmother and how Zionism fortified her sense of home. Beinart's

framing narrative sets the stage for the rest of his book; this first-person strategy composes a

sense of self-understanding in relation to the larger Israel-Palestine conflict. As I will

demonstrate, this rhetorical practice becomes a form of persuasive self-representation. A

strategic presentation of the self can function as an argument, address, and appeal to examine an

issue that is larger than the self but which the self still embodies in a different way.

So, what happens when something, someone, or a situation interrupts one's sense of self, calling into question the foundation of one's identity? Although *The Crisis of Zionism* begins with Beinart's personal narrative about his grandmother and family history, he presents another coinciding story, where he reflects on a video that he saw online:

> In the video, Israeli police drag Fadel [Fadel Jaber, a West Bank Palestinian man] toward some kind of paddy wagon. And then the camera pans down, to a five-year-old boy with a striped shirt and short brown hair, Khaled, who is frantically trying to navigate the thicket of adults in order to reach his father. As his father is pulled away, he keeps screaming, 'Baba, Baba.'

> As soon as I began watching the video, I wished I had never turned it on. For most of my life, my reaction to accounts of Palestinian suffering has been rationalization, a search for reasons why the accounts are exaggerated or the suffering self-inflicted. In that respect, I suspect, I'm like many American Jews. But in recent years, for reasons I can't fully explain, I had been lowering my defenses, and Khaled's cries left me staring in mute horror at my computer screen. (3)

Afterward, Beinart contextualizes the video, explaining that Fadel was arrested because he tried to connect his Palestinian village to water pipes that ran through a nearby Jewish settlement and Israeli military base.[47] Citing the Israeli human rights organization B'Tselem, Beinart writes that Israeli Jewish settlers use about five times as much water per person compared to West Bank

---

[47] About Fadel's case, the Israeli news site *+972 Magazine* reported: "Israel has constructed water pipes in the area, but they only serve the army and the settlers. The Palestinians are forced to drive to the closest town, and buy their water in tanks over there. They end up paying 10 times the price I pay in Tel Aviv. And the farmers in South mount Hebron are the poorest of the Palestinian population. They live in tents, some even in caves. They used to have water holes in which they stored rain waters, but access to their fields and to many of the holes in them is denied by the army and the settlers. [...] With no other option, some farmers were forced to use unauthorized connections to the Israeli water system, running just a few meters from their tents" (Sheizaf).

Palestinians, who "fall far below the World Health Organization's recommended daily water consumption rate" (3).

In *Parting Ways: Jewishness and the Critique of Zionism*, Butler illustrates a type of transformation that occurs when the self responds to the demands of alterity or what happens when discourse from the disavowed Other becomes audible to the self. Butler theorizes that such an encounter between the self and foreign Other serves to disrupt one's identity, expose the self, and acts as a dispossession from one's prior standing. Butler argues for the revival of Jewish exilic tradition as a modality of ethical relation, which simultaneously becomes the ground for hearing the demand of alterity with its unsettling familiarity *and* a dispossession from that shared ground, which is both familiar and alien, to defamiliarize the familiar. Similarly, rhetorician Diane Davis theorizes such an encounter between self and foreign Other as a disruption of identity, an exposedness of the self. In the ethical relation with alterity, the ego shatters, and the face of the Other demands a rhetorical responsibility to heed the demand—a "response-ability." Davis argues, "The relation with the face, then, is itself nonviolent yet expropriating: to encounter a face is to be both called into question and into service. As pure affective appeal, the face subjects one to the scandal of obligation in which ego, finding itself compelled to respond, is stripped of its sense of self-mastery and spontaneity" (13, 14). Davis contends that this pure affectivity is itself a type of rhetoricity that precedes the symbolic or is the condition of possibility for the symbolic as such.

While Beinart tells the story of Fadel, a disenfranchised, stateless Palestinian father, who lives in the West Bank, he interrupts his personal narrative as a self-identified Jewish Zionist, U.S. citizen, and father. According to Butler, to *interrupt* means, "something happens to the 'subject' that dislocates it from the center of the world; some demand from elsewhere lays claim to me, presses itself upon me, or even divides me from within, and only through this fissuring of who I am do I stand a chance of relating to another" (*Parting* 6). Beinart not only recounts the scene of interruption, but he is compelled to do so; his first-person narrative of the events is delivered as a testimony about what he witnessed on-screen, although he "wished [he] had never turned it on" (3). Rhetorician Michael Bernard-Donals argues, "To be called, then, is to see or hear some aspect of reality, as it has been made manifest through discourse or as it *interrupts* discourse, that does not let you go, or that you cannot let go of, and that challenges what you thought you knew" ("The Call" 400, *original emphasis*). Beinart observes the recorded event, hears the call of the oppressed, and feels compelled to respond and retell the story as a witness.

In this retelling, Beinart is listening to the demand coming from the Palestinian Other, while also reinventing his Jewish identity during the process. In the dominant strains of Zionist ideology, the Jewish nation-state is highly valued, and the end goal of state formation is justified by the means. In his break with dominant Zionist framing, Beinart returns to religious tradition to reinvent his self-understanding in relation to alterity. He draws upon the deep cultural reservoir of Jewish values concerning justice and witnessing suffering. On *The Crisis of Zionism*'s book cover, the title design is cracked beneath shattered glass, which Beinart chose to exemplify Jewish traditional symbolism in his dissent concerning Israel and Palestine. In the Jewish ritual of a wedding ceremony, breaking glass symbolizes not only the destruction of Jerusalem's Second Temple but also the shattering of the soul before birth and the reunification of the soul with one's marriage partner under the *chuppah*.

From the opening scene, Beinart defends Israel as a Jewish state and democracy throughout his book because he fears it will succumb to the West Bank's annexation and the collapse of the Israeli democracy into a segregated nation between stateless Palestinians and

Israeli citizens. Beinart's defense of Israeli democracy is also a critique of political power as an end in and of itself. Just as the traditional shattering of glass returns the soul, in his first-person narrative, Beinart's ego shatters and departs from his dominant political Zionism that had preconceived the Palestinian Other as a threat, an antisemitic terrorist, or a self-inflicted victim. Instead, he returns to Jewish values and religious tradition by reinventing his identity in relation to human suffering.

For Beinart, the crux of interruption arrives when he hears five-year-old Khaled screaming, "*Baba*" (see fig. 2). The demand of the foreign Other came from Khaled, as Beinart explains his personal connection was due to his having a four-year-old son at the time, who also called him, "*Baba.*" According to Burke's theories of identification and alchemic opportunities for transformation, it is precisely the familiar that causes Beinart to open up to the unfamiliar in a moment of ambiguity (e.g., a feeling of confusion, distress, déjà vu, or sensing the uncanny), where the subject is dislocated from their prior standing. In this transformative opportunity, Beinart's first-person narrative exhibits a shift toward having an ethical relationship to alterity. In his first-person identity constitution, which Beinart describes in the beginning, Zionism is positioned as the ideal in his life's narrative. He weaves his life story alongside his grandmother's, from whom he says he inherited a particular version of Zionism that represents safety, rootedness, and home, which had been established after centuries of his family's continued dispossession in the larger history of antisemitism.

Fig. 2. Fadel Jaber arrested for "stealing water" (Sheizaf; photo: Noam Sheizaf).

The first-person identity constitution that appeared fixed had become blurred, and in the scene of interruption after "recent years, for reasons [he] can't fully explain, [he] had been lowering [his] defenses," (3) Beinart's preconceived notions of Zionism are deeply challenged. This moment of ambiguity engenders a self-reconstitution of identity in relation to Palestinian rights. This is not necessarily an epiphany (i.e., an isolated before-and-after incident), but rather, it exists as a turning point in the attunement process. It illustrates how the demand of alterity becomes audible to the self. In this particular context, the suffering of the disavowed Palestinian Other becomes audible after years of "lowering defenses" due to a specific interruption of identity that initiated a redefinition of Jewish self-understanding in regard to the State of Israel.

In his rhetorical use of first-person narrative, Beinart invites what is arguably his Jewish target audience to reflect on this moment of ambiguity with him. In a way, Beinart concedes his tightly held prior position when he says, "For most of my life, my reaction to accounts of Palestinian suffering has been rationalization, a search for reasons why the accounts are exaggerated or the suffering self-inflicted" (3). He feels he can no longer rationalize the suffering of the Palestinian Other. His use of the first-person narrative as rhetorical strategy illustrates that reconciliation in Israel and Palestine is not only about land and sovereignty, but it also concerns identity and collective self-understanding. Sara Roy's first-person narrative further demonstrates a reinvented identity in relation to Palestinian rights through the symbolism of shared histories concerning dispossession as well as Jewish values of justice and the sanctity of home.

I want to emphasize that the significance of this research involves dissenters that are not only breaking the silence over the dominant discourse but are proposing a different way of thinking about Jewish self-understanding. How does a multi-ethnic, inclusive Israel and Palestine appear? Butler's conception of an ethical relationship to alterity in the context of the Israel-Palestine connection causes the reinvention of Jewish self-identity, which relinquishes Zionist interpretations of Jewish suffering (i.e., the myth of Holocaust and Redemption). Instead, it draws upon diasporic tradition to reconstitute identity in relation to the Other in exile. Drawing upon the work of Said, Butler argues that "diasporic existence is constituted in the midst of cultural heterogeneity, negotiating difference, indeed affirming difference or plurality as a condition of its own existence" (*Parting* 215). In this way, the Jewish tradition of identifying as wanderers, exiles, and refugees has become a cultural resource to connect with the foreign Other, who is also experiencing diaspora. Having shared histories of dispossession and dispersion has become a shared experience that enables identification as well as identity's transformation. To welcome the stranger is to welcome the self; the Jewish self is considered the stranger, just as Palestinians have been made the stranger in their homeland and in diaspora communities around the world.

Reframing the Zionist Mythos of Rebirth and Redemption

Sara Roy's essay, "Living with the Holocaust: The Journey of a Child of Holocaust Survivors," immediately opens by connecting her self-understanding as a child of Holocaust survivors to the Israel-Palestine conflict and what it means to be Jewish: "Though I cannot possibly say everything, it seems especially poignant that I should be addressing this topic at a time when the conflict between Israelis and Palestinians is descending so tragically into a moral abyss and when, for me at least, the very essence of Judaism, of what it means to be a Jew, seems to be descending with it" (5). When Roy first delivered this essay at Baylor University on April 8, 2002 for the Second Annual Holocaust Remembrance Lecture, the military operation, Operation Defensive Shield, had begun ten days earlier, which was the largest in the West Bank since the 1967 Six-Day War. The Second Palestinian Intifada, or uprising, began in September 2000, and it lasted until February 2005.

Whereas the First Intifada (1987–1993), which predated and precipitated the Oslo Accords peace negotiations (1993–2000), is characterized by its widespread grassroots mobilization efforts, the Second Intifada was—in many ways—the corollary of Oslo's entrenched Israeli occupation along the West Bank and Gaza Strip. Not only has the outcome of the peace negotiations *not* been peaceful, but matters have become increasingly intractable. On the brink of this failure, the Second Intifada was marked by Palestinian suicide bombings and Israel's overwhelming militarized response with tanks, air attacks, and numerous targeted killings. In this context, Roy laments that "the conflict between Israelis and Palestinians is descending so tragically into a moral abyss" ("Living" 5).

Roy organizes the first-person narrative of her journey, as a child of Holocaust survivors, by describing first encounters and the defining moments of her life. She illustrates varying identifications and identity changes that take shape through self-definitions and scene-act ratios. Instead of understanding Roy's narrative as a before-and-after transformation, I observe it as a story of self-understanding in relation to significant personal and historical events, which dialectically challenge and (re)orientate her constitutional principles. Roy establishes the arc of her story through two distinct, yet interrelated, first encounters involving the Holocaust and the Israeli occupation. The centerpiece of Roy's narrative unites these two encounters in a reflective moment that encapsulates the overall aim of her argument:

> In this critical respect, my first encounter with the occupation was the same as my first encounter with the Holocaust, with the number on my father's arm. It spoke the same message: the denial of one's humanity. It is important to understand the very real differences in volume, scale, and horror between the Holocaust and the occupation and to be careful about comparing the two, but it is also important to recognize parallels where they do exist. ("Living" 9)

Although Roy experiences moral shock that influences her self-constitution, her story is not a conversion that renders a dramatic reorientation from Zionist to anti-Zionist, like some narratives in this larger rhetorical corpus.[48] Instead, I argue that Roy's rhetoric of identity is a disruption in the hegemonic framing of the Holocaust and Israeli occupation. Under this dominant framework, Israeli security rhetoric justifies the status quo of occupation in the name of self-defense against the existential threat of a second holocaust.

In her narrative, Roy experiences Holocaust memories that were shared by family members and the Israeli occupation in various ways that direct her identity's constitutional principles to fulfill her sense of self. She becomes a witness to the Other's suffering, and through this recognition, she identifies with the Other in terms of their shared history of dispossession. Whereas the dominant Israeli and American shared framework understands the Arab Other as an

---

[48] See Karcher, ed., *Stories of Personal Transformation: Reclaiming Judaism from Zionism* for a compelling collection of first-person narratives about the reorientation of Jewish Zionist identity to alternative forms of Zionism, non-Zionism, and anti-Zionism.)

antisemitic existential threat, Roy's rhetoric of identity reframes this relationship to the Palestinian Other as being co-constitutive historical realities that transcend national boundaries. Specifically, she turns to the Israeli-Palestinian, Arab-Jewish shared symbolism of the home and the sanctity of its physical space to transpose the dominant discourse into a "coarticulation with alterity" (Butler, *Parting* 30). Historian Nadim Khoury writes, "Deliberations on memory are public discussions between members of divided societies aimed at transforming their respective national narratives. … The goal of these deliberations is to find resources in history and memory to promote an alternative future between both people" (114). For her audience at the Holocaust Remembrance Lecture, Roy offers a counternarrative to the dominant Zionist mythos by reconnecting the tragedy of the Holocaust to the Palestinians' fate.

For Roy, the language of the Holocaust (e.g., its lessons and remembrances) creates a sense of Judaism that is reaffirmed as an ethical relationship to the oppressed through values, such as "bearing witness, railing against injustice and foregoing silence" as well as "compassion, tolerance, and rescue" ("Living" 7). In the periphery of Roy's personal narrative, the Holocaust functions as an ideal that defines her self-constitution: "The Holocaust has been the *defining feature* of my life. It could not have been otherwise. I lost over 100 members of my family and extended family in the Nazi ghettos and death camps in Poland" ("Living" 5, *emphasis added*). Not only did her maternal grandparents perish, but Roy's mother and two of her aunts, including one who immigrated to Palestine in 1936, were only three out of nine siblings that survived the Holocaust. It is not necessarily the Holocaust that defines Roy's ultimate motivation to construct a first-person identity, but rather, the Holocaust serves as a metaphor or cultural reservoir of resources, which she can draw from to reaffirm Jewish traditions.

Roy enmeshes her journey with the life stories of her family members (e.g., her mother, father, and extended family), especially concerning her connection to the Jewish tradition of justice for all. Hence, Roy is not simply recounting a family story within the typical conventions of a biography that straightforwardly narrates the chronological developments of a lived experience. Rather, as she weaves her personal journey into the stories of her family, Roy argues for the reemergence of Jewish tradition, which has been subsumed and negated by dominant Zionist politics and the Israeli occupation. Roy characterizes three defining, interrelated principles of her upbringing that portray her identity and speak to larger ideas concerning "what it means to be a Jew," especially in light of the Holocaust and State of Israel ("Living" 5).

Roy's first constitutional principle is "to live as a Jew in a pluralist society." She directly associates this principle with her mother, who made the life-changing decision to move to the United States instead of Israel after the war: "She told me many times during my life that her decision not to live in Israel was based on a belief, learned and reinforced by her experiences during the war, that tolerance, compassion, and justice cannot be practiced or extended when one lives only among one's own" ("Living" 7). This connects to her second principle, which is defined by what it is not: "Obedience to a state was not an ultimate Jewish value, not for them [Roy's parents], not after the Holocaust. Judaism provided the context for our life and for values and beliefs that were not dependent upon national boundaries, but transcended them" ("Living" 7). Thus, to restate her second principle in positive terms, it refers to transcending national boundaries. Thirdly, Roy learns from her parents to "confront what [she] did not know or understand. Noam Chomsky speaks of the 'parameters of thinkable thought'," and for Roy, her third constitutive command involves pushing these parameters as far as she can and understand "the importance of doing so" ("Living" 7).

As a young adult, Roy's personal relationship to Israel involves contradiction, as she struggles with in her Jewish identity. This path leads her to pursue a doctoral dissertation about America's economic assistance that was given to the West Bank and Gaza Strip. While Roy visited Israel many times before, she first visits the occupied Palestinian territories in the summer of 1985 for fieldwork as a graduate student: "That summer changed my life because it was then that I came to understand and experience what occupation was and what it meant" ("Living" 8). Through the scene-act ratios, Roy illustrates the significant changes in her sense of identity and begins to establish the conflict between what it means to be Jewish regarding Jewish statehood. These changes elicit her to rewrite her self-understanding, as a child of Holocaust survivors.

Roy recalls one of her first encounters with the occupation when she witnessed Israeli soldiers harassing an elderly Palestinian man with a small child, who was walking a donkey. The soldiers verbally harassed the man about the donkey's yellow teeth: "Don't you brush your donkey's teeth?" Eventually, this behavior culminated to the soldiers yelling at the man about his donkey, causing the child to cry while the elderly man stood silently in humiliation. Roy remembers that she stood "in stunned disbelief," and she "immediately thought of the stories [her] parents had told [her] of how Jews had been treated by the Nazis in the 1930s, before the ghettos and death camps," especially how they were harassed and deliberately humiliated in public. Roy argues, "What happened to the old man was absolutely equivalent in principle, intent, and impact: to humiliate and dehumanize" ("Living" 9).

In *Holocaust Images and Picturing Catastrophe*, media scholar Angi Buettner references Roy's 2002 Holocaust Remembrance Lecture: "In a post-Holocaust world, […] the Holocaust is used as a mode of representation to make visible the suffering and the need to repair injustice." Buettner contends that for Roy, the Holocaust is used as "a rhetorical strategy to make visible what we would prefer not to see [...] in order to get attention and turn attention to an other" (41).

Furthermore, Roy evokes Jewish traditions and lessons from her parents as the lens to recognize

the suffering of the foreign Other and understand her sense of self. Thus, she reinvents Jewish

identity apart from dominant Zionist dispositions, as she moves toward coarticulating shared

histories of dispossession and dehumanization.

In addition to what happened to the elderly man, Roy recalls watching Palestinian

families standing on the sidelines, sobbing and screaming, as Israeli militarized bulldozers

demolished their houses and everything within. Israeli martial law justifies demolitions like this

when Palestinians build their houses without acquiring official Israeli permits first. However,

with only a few permits granted annually, many Palestinians have no choice but to build without

official authorization. Roy argues, "It is perhaps in the concept of home and shelter that I find the

most profound link between the Jews and the Palestinians and, perhaps, the most painful

illustration of the meaning of occupation" (10). Roy quotes the Israeli historian Meron

Benvenisti, concerning Palestinian society and the "symbolic value of a house," coarticulating a

sense of shared tradition with the Other: "The arrival of a firstborn son and the building of a

home are the central events in such an individual's life because they symbolize continuity in time

and physical space. And with the demolition of the individual's home comes the destruction of

the world" (Benvenisti qtd. in Roy, "Living" 10). The symbolism of the home and the tragedy of

its destruction for Palestinians deeply resonates in accordance with Jewish tradition, which can

be depicted in a commonly cited verse from the Mishnah (the Oral Torah): "Therefore was a

single human being created: to teach you that to destroy a single human soul is equivalent to

destroying an entire world; and that to sustain a single human soul is equivalent to sustaining an

entire world" (Stern 5). As she cites Benvenisti, Roy invites her audience to make this poignant connection, which further exemplifies her utilization of Jewish tradition in the reinvention of

identity in relation to Palestinian rights.

The Agonism of Identity

Holocaust-centered Israeli security rhetoric indicates that Israel is under attack by

antisemitic terrorism and that Israel has no choice but to defend itself. The threat becomes

existential as civilizations clash in an "us versus them" scenario. By speaking out against the

Israeli occupation, Roy reframes Holocaust remembrance and composes Jewish identity in terms

of a pluralist society, and she incorporates Jewish traditions of justice that bear witness to

suffering. While the respective narratives of Roy and Beinart exhibit self-understanding that is

reconstituted apart from dominant Zionist mythos, their personal definitions of themselves are

also outwardly directed to shape and respond to the situation that implicates their identities. In

her self-reconstitution of identity in the context of significant historical and personal life events,

Roy interweaves a first-person narrative with family history, Holocaust memory, and the tragedy

of the Israel-Palestine conflict, including a discussion about Jewish-Arab, Palestinian-Israeli

shared symbolism that involves the sanctity of life and home.

Butler argues that an ethical relation to alterity requires a sense of self-understanding that

surpasses the confines of nationalism and insular identity "as defining frameworks. It establishes

the relation to alterity as constitutive of identity, which is to say that the relation to alterity

interrupts identity, and this interruption is the condition of ethical relationality" (*Parting* 5). In

this sense, as part of the agonism of identity, interruption is identity's rhetorical nature, meaning

that identity is never fixed nor final but inherently ambiguous in its performative enactment of

constitutional wishes and ideals. The point of identity is not to achieve a final ideal state, but for the ideal to guide the unending process of identity as a mode for developing ethical relations. Identity's performative enactment is ultimately imperfect, in that every act is one "of hierarchizing or prioritizing; every act is also an act of determining which principle reigns at any given time, for no single act can honor all that is willed in a constitution's concept of substance" (Anderson 85). For Butler, a modality for having an ethical relation to alterity requires a disposition that is open to the unfamiliar, "even a willingness to cede ground to what is not immediately knowable within established epistemological fields" (*Parting* 12). Beinart and Roy differentially transpose the terms of unquestioned pro-Israel support into a narrative framework that regards the self-determination of a stranger as being bound up with one's fate.

In this chapter, I have demonstrated the necessity of a rhetorical theory approach to justice and peacemaking in the Israel-Palestine conflict. What I am suggesting implicates a profound change in Jewish identity *in relation to* Israel by reframing Zionist conceptions of the Palestinian Other. How can further research address the transformative possibilities of such change that is currently happening? Roy reframes the terrorist threat to recognize the tragedy of the Holocaust by connecting it to the fate of Palestinians; Beinart reframes the Palestinian Other as a self-inflicted victim by promoting an ethical relation that necessitates interdependent responsibility. Roy and Beinart each utilize first-person narratives to disrupt the dominant discourse that attaches the threat of antisemitism to exclusionary modes of ethnic nationalism.

At the heart of this reinvention of identity, American Jewish dissenters must necessarily reframe the threat of antisemitism *in relation to* (rather than separately from) other forms of dehumanization. Not only are Beinart and Roy appealing to other Jews—in this breaking of accepted protocol—by speaking out against the Israeli occupation in support of Palestinian rights, but they also refuse to reject the Jewish community and their inclusion. Therefore, through the reconstitution of their Jewish self-understanding, which is apart from dominant Zionist mentalities, Roy and Beinart are working to redraw the contours of first-person identity constitutions to create space for dissident voices to become legible within the larger community.

through the reconstitution of their Jewish self-understanding, which is apart from dominant Zionist mentalities, Roy and Beinart are working to redraw the contours of first-person identity constitutions to create space for dissident voices to become legible within the larger community.

Chapter 4

Rhetorical Refusal of Birthright and the Universal Jewish Audience

Fig. 3. Student activist holds a sign for the #ReturnTheBirthright campaign ("Young Jews"; photo: Nesha Ruther).

In the #ReturnTheBirthright campaign, Jewish student activists enact dissociative moves in their political rhetoric that extend the principle of self-determination away from the insular logic of ethnonationalism and toward the values of inclusivity and justice for all. In a photo on the campaign website (see fig. 3), protester Nesha Ruther at the University of Wisconsin-Madison holds a sign that reads: "I return the Birthright because everyone should be able to go HOME!" ("Young Jews"). Through this declarative refusal, Ruther rejects the idea of exclusionary birthright by disrupting the value hierarchy that solely privileges the Jewish as belonging in Israel. She then reinvents the concept of birthright in an appeal to the language of self-determination for all humans' right to have a right to their home. By "everyone," Ruther also means the Palestinian people, millions who wish to return to their homes inside Israel but cannot because they are not Jewish. Her declaration functions as an act of solidarity in support of Palestinian rights, because Ruther is, in effect, including Palestinians in her self-reconstitution of her Jewish identity with regard to her right of return. In this way, her refusal seeks to expand the definitional concept of who is included in the universal Jewish audience. By incorporating Palestinians, she radically reshapes this audience in an act of self-dispossession.

In Perelmanian rhetorical theory, the universal audience is a construct of an author or speaker; it is a largely symbolic, rational being who one addresses and to whom one makes their case (Gross 203–204). Universal audiences are therefore definitional concepts that rhetors seek to uphold, challenge, or expand on from the position of a particular audience. Particular audiences are situated in specific sociohistorical contexts and take shape across an array of rhetorical situations through intersections of race, religion, gender, sexuality, ethnicity, class, disability, nationality, citizenship status, and so on. In this way, the universal audience becomes political because it constructs and advocates for certain conceptions of the real. Rhetorician Antonio Raul de Velasco shows how universality as a norm or ideal can circulate to reinforce hegemonic relations. The universal audience then appears apolitical through the naturalization of the dominant ideology as the taken for granted reality (de Velasco 60–61). Through dissociation, a particular audience can question the ideal and "advance its expanded notion of what constitutes the universal audience" (Fernheimer 62). Dissociation is a two-step maneuver whereby a rhetor first breaks the links in a concept or idea then restructures that concept in new or alternative ways (Perelman and Olbrechts-Tyteca 411–413). While dissociation is a forceful way to expand or recast constitutional terms of the real, it is risky — a dominant group may not engage a marginalized group's break in terms or accept its reformulated value hierarchy (Fernheimer 63–

64). Nonetheless, this reframed worldview reimagines who or what forms the universal audience of that community.

In her study of the 1971 Black Jewish identity conflict, Fernheimer conceptualizes the "universal Jewish audience" as a definitional category of group self-understanding (50). Fernheimer contextualizes the value hierarchies that recognize Jewish identity status in terms of *halacha* (Jewish law based on the Talmud) in conjunction with Israel's Law of Return.[49] She notes, "Some argue the price of Jewish normalcy is purchased on the back of Palestinian persecution, but a full discussion of the Palestinian-Israeli situation and the larger Arab-Israeli conflict is beyond the scope of this article" (57n24). In this chapter, I widen the scope of the universal Jewish audience by examining it as an ethnonationalist construct that reproduces itself through the disavowal of Palestinian identity and history. In the #ReturnTheBirthright and #NotJustAFreeTrip campaigns, student activists' reinvented concept of birthright expands the universal Jewish audience to incorporate Palestinian rights. These features of their reinvented audience envision a binational rhetoric of belonging for both Israelis and Palestinians.

As I discussed in chapter two, ethnonationalism, taken to its logical conclusion, believes in ethnic purity and supremacy and the right to sovereignty for the presumed homogenous group. For dominant Zionist ideology, a militarized homeland in the name of security against the antisemitic existential threat of another holocaust was and remains the only answer. Rowland and Frank argue that ethnonationalist fundamentalisms are entelechial, which explains the willingness to use violence in order to achieve the end of mythic perfection. Rowland and Frank define entelechy as a "symbolic force that causes humans to extend an idea to the 'end of the line' in search of perfection, which often produces terrible results" ("Mythic" 43). Dominant

---

[49] Jewish birthright to Israeli citizenship.

Zionism is a territorial maximalist project that believes that all of the land on both sides of the Jordan River to the Mediterranean Sea belongs to the Jews, called "Greater Israel." Within this frame, Palestinian resistance to Israeli occupation becomes an existential threat, a daily danger to the security of the state embodied by the antisemitic Arab terrorist Other.[50] As I have illustrated thus far, dominant Zionist ideology relies on rhetorical moves such as decontextualization (no mention of the military occupation, home invasions and demolitions, disenfranchisement, arbitrary detentions), the villain–hero–victim drama triangle, mythic claims to sacred land, the negation of Palestinian history and identity, and the linkage of modern-day struggle to a heroic past of righteous ancestors.

The struggle for justice against exclusionary ethnonationalisms and Israeli apartheid is playing out across American universities. College campuses have become a site of contestation regarding Israeli apartheid and Palestinian rights. In the dominant American and Israeli shared frame, Palestinian rights activism on college campuses is seen as contributing to a hostile environment for Jewish students that can cross the line into antisemitism. Israeli politician Natan Sharansky is known for his "3D Test" about antisemitism directed at Israel. Many Israel advocates utilize this framework and argue that when Zionism is deemed a form of racism (codified as such in the IHRA definition of antisemitism), for example, this meets all three "Ds" of the test: Israel is being demonized, delegitimized, and held to a double standard.[51] The implication of this premise is that the State of Israel comes to stand in for the Jewish people. In this frame, universities are a "battleground" of anti-Israel animus where Jewish students feel threatened (Cohen 91). Despite this belief, recent studies from Stanford University and Brandeis

---

[50] As I've discussed, the Palestinian population is also considered a demographic threat to Israel's Jewish character and existence.

[51] For further theorizing of this framework, see also: Wistrich, "Anti-Zionism and Anti-Semitism."

University have found that Jewish students feel safe and welcome at school (see Kelman, et al,

and Wright et al). In one of their key findings from the Brandeis study, Wright et al contend:

"The majority of students disagree that there is a hostile environment toward Israel on campus"

(1). Nevertheless, in the "3D Test" interpretive frame, the rise of Palestinian rights activism on

campus becomes conflated with anti-Israel animus and antisemitism. In effect, this 3D

framework not only deflects the substance of claims from Palestinian perspectives but also stifles

dissent with the charge of antisemitism in what has come to be called "the weaponization of

antisemitism."[52]

Although criticism of Israel is regarded as antisemitic by dominant Zionist ideology,

dissent in support of Palestinian rights in American public discourse is shifting from its

historically marginalized position to a more widely accepted and legitimized view (Roy,

"Reflections" 24–25).[53] For American Jews, Waxman attributes this shift to generational

---

[52] See Friedman, "Weaponizing Anti-Semitism, State Department Delegitimizes Human Rights Groups"; Jacobs, et al, "Fighting Anti-Semitism and its Weaponization in American Politics"; and Stern, "I drafted the definition of antisemitism. Rightwing Jews are weaponizing it."

[53] The first decade of the twenty-first century laid the grounds for legitimizing dissent. Roy attributes this change to several factors. She contends that although post-9/11 U.S.-Israel discourse reconsolidated the stereotype of the Arab terrorist threat, "arguing with great effect that it is not Israel's occupation that causes terrorism but terrorism that necessitates the occupation," there was still the beginning of a shift in debate with the 2003 U.S. invasion of Iraq, the end of the Second Intifada, and American activist Rachel Corrie's tragic death by an IDF armored bulldozer while protesting the demolition of a Palestinian home. At this time, more academics, analysts, and activists began openly questioning the role of the U.S. in the Middle East including Israel and Palestine. Israeli public figures in the Knesset and military and intelligence community also began to question the nature of Israeli democracy. Roy argues that the work of such outspoken Israeli officials has been undeniably essential to "creating a substantive foundation for subsequent intellectual and political challenges. It also has given U.S. Jews who care about Israel permission to criticize it" ("Reflections" 25). In 2007, then-Secretary of State Condoleezza Rice "compared conditions in the occupied territories to segregation" (Roy, "Reflections" 26), and around the same time Jimmy Carter's book *Palestine: Peace Not Apartheid*, and John Mearsheimer and Stephen Walt's *The Israel Lobby*, constituted significant interventions in public discourse about U.S. support of Israeli policies.
   Since the turn of the century, there have also been high-profile cases of academic freedom and the question of Palestine involving scholars such as Norman Finkelstein, Joseph Massad, Nadia Abu El-Haj, Wadie Said, and Steven Salaita (see Abraham, *Out of Bounds: Academic Freedom and the Question of Palestine*). Writing in 2010, Roy argues, "People can still lose their jobs in academia or government for speaking critically of Israeli policies, but it is no longer as axiomatic as it once was. The capacity and willingness to resist and defend have grown enormously" ("Reflections" 28). In addition, Roy argues that there has been a cultural shift in media and movies, seen in productions such as the 2009 CBS *60 Minutes* segment "Is Peace Out of Reach?" with reporter Bob Simon that depicted a highly critical investigation into the Israeli occupation and settlement project. The same year, prominent Palestinian activist Mustafa Barghouti and Jewish American peace activist Anna Baltzar made an

memory. He contends that today's Jewish college students "are much more likely than their

parents or grandparents to be exposed to the Palestinian narrative [and this] might be one reason

why they tend to be more dovish in their opinions about the Israeli-Palestinian conflict"

("Young" 185). In terms of Israel-themed programming, Rabbi Leah Cohen maintains that the

overused "campus battleground" metaphor deters students from interest because it "perpetuates

an obsession with crisis as the primary paradigm for engaging with Israel" (92). Moreover,

Cohen writes, "They [Jewish students] are shocked to learn about Palestinians and a more

multifaceted version of Israel's history that includes aspects they have never heard about

growing up. This subset of the Jewish student population is often very angry and feels deceived

by their parents, teachers, and rabbis" (94). She argues that students are more interested in a

critical thinking approach to Israel education than an advocacy approach.

Exposure to the Palestinian narrative leads Jewish student dissenters to reinvent their self-

understanding and relationship with Israel as a co-articulation with their Palestinian neighbors. In

the #ReturnTheBirthright and #NotJustAFreeTrip campaigns, Jewish student activists no longer

relate to Israel without incorporating consideration of native Palestinian Arabs, who view the

same piece of land as their ancestral home. Moreover, upon critical reflection on the role of

contemporary Jewish power and privilege in relation to the stateless Palestinian people, this co-

articulation of identity should be understood as asymmetrical.

When social justice activists intervene in hegemonic narratives in an effort to reinvent the

imagined universal audience of that community, supporters of the dominant view may or may

not accept their appeal to higher moral ground. Disrupting Zionist constructions of Jewish

---

appearance on *The Daily Show* with Jon Stewart. Major film festivals such as the San Francisco Jewish Film
Festival started screening otherwise controversial movies and documentaries about Palestinian rights. The Internet
has also played a crucial role in shifting public discourse about equal rights and occupation in Israel and Palestine.

identity and redrawing the contours of the universal audience as a co-articulation with the Palestinian Other entails significant risk. Perelman and Olbrechts-Tyteca contend, "The elite audience embodies the universal audience only for those who acknowledge this role of vanguard and model. For the rest it will be no more than a particular audience" (34). #ReturnTheBirthright and #NotJustAFreeTrip activists thus risk being dismissed as "no more than a particular audience" in their hope that some may accept the campaigns' break in protocol and see this cultural work as a vanguard and model for future deliberation. I examine the campaigns' rhetoric because I see the activists' work in the role of vanguard in the way they uproot the entrenched logics of Zionist narratives and reinvent the concept of birthright for all. Jewish student activists reconstitute the universal audience with an appeal to justice that integrates Palestinian rights into Jewish self-understanding. In this fashion, the #NotJustAFreeTrip and #ReturnTheBirthright campaigns redraw the boundaries of permissible political speech through dissociative moves that disrupt ethnonationalist notions of universality.

Four Demands for Birthright

In June 2018, five American Jewish activists walked off their Birthright trip in Israel in protest of Israel's occupation of the West Bank. In addition to this tactic, student activists began meeting Birthright participants at their airport of departure to talk with them about the Israeli occupation of the West Bank and blockade of the Gaza Strip. Taglit-Birthright is a nonprofit educational organization that sponsors free ten-day trips to Israel for young Jewish adults. It has sponsored over 750,000 participants since its founding in 1999. The Hebrew word *taglit* means "discovery" — therefore, the program's itinerary aims to create a thought-provoking and affective experience of self-discovery in participants, one which connects their self-understanding of their Jewish identity to the State of Israel.[54] Political scientist Yehonatan

Abramson argues, "The history offered during such tours often tends to essentialize the ethnic

group, excluding others who do not share the territory, the history, or the eligibility to participate

in these tours" (16). Sociologists Leonard Saxe and Barry Chazan contend that Birthright offers

an apolitical and immersive educational itinerary for young Jews to learn about Judaism and

connect with Israel, where trip participants are exposed to a "range of views held by Israeli

Jews" (not Palestinians) (50).

In chapter one, I examined how Zionist ideology reformulated Jewish religious tradition

into this-worldly secular terms. Early political Zionists called for national self-emancipation and

the swift ingathering of exiles into territorial concentration in Palestine. Drawing upon the deep

reservoirs of Jewish ritual that long for return to Jerusalem and celebrate liberation from

bondage, Zionism continues to refashion exilic tradition into what anthropologist Jonathan

Boyarin calls "the territorialization of identity" (218) or what Zerubavel terms "the primacy of

the people-land bond" (16). In Zionist reconstructions of the past, Zerubavel contends that the

people-land bond sees Israel, the modern-day nation-state, as a miraculous return to the land of

ancient Israelite kingdoms (22–23). Zionist rhetoric also believes that the Land of Israel is a

God-given biblical mandate. Various strains of Zionism in more secular terms take this ancient

history as the Jewish people's "historical right" to the land—hence, the notion of birthright.

Saxe and Chazan draw a connection between the ancient Land of Canaan to "present-day

Israel" and suggest that the first "'Birthright Israel' trip" takes place in the Book of Genesis by

Abraham, who travels from Ur to Canaan in Parshat Lech Lecha. Saxe and Chazan argue,

---

[54] The Birthright website states: "Our hope is that our trips motivate young people to continue to explore their Jewish identity and support for Israel and maintain long-lasting connections with the Israelis they meet on their trip" ("Our Goals").

"Birthright Israel participants are repeatedly reminded that they are in a country with rich historical roots reaching back to the Bible" (23). Their research also shows how Birthright trips illustrate the significance of Israel's existence as a safe haven for Jews after atrocities such as the Holocaust. Saxe and Chazan write, "*Mi-Shoah L'Tkuma* (from Holocaust to renewal) is a central Birthright Israel theme. Israel, though a modern democracy, remains the refuge of the Jewish people and the guarantor of the survival of the Jewish people" (49–50). Saxe and Chazan contend that Birthright inspires a commitment to Israel as a guarantor of Jewish continuity.

JVP's #ReturnTheBirthright and IfNotNow's #NotJustAFreeTrip both speak directly to would-be Birthright participants, Birthright alumni, the larger organization itself, to the U.S. Jewish establishment and mainstream community, and by extension to Zionist discourse more broadly regarding the notion of Jewish birthright to Israel. In a testimonial published in *The Nation*, walk-off activist and graduate student Bethany Zaiman explains that the Birthright map of "Greater Israel" handed out on tours does not mark the boundaries of the occupied West Bank. She writes, "Looking at the map, I was taken aback by the blatant way this supposedly apolitical trip was making such a political decision as to erase the existence of Palestinian people and their land. I felt something inside of me break, and I knew I needed to do something" (Zaiman). Zaiman and other walk-offs joined a different tour led by Breaking the Silence, a nonprofit run by Israeli veterans who speak out about their service in the West Bank in hopes of ending the occupation.

Today, between the West Bank, Israel, and the Gaza Strip, there are approximately thirteen million people, about half of whom are Palestinian Arabs, the other half being Israeli Jews. Three million Palestinians live under Israeli military occupation in the West Bank and two million live in Gaza under a land, air, and sea blockade imposed by Israel and Egypt. In the West

Bank, there are two separate laws for two different peoples. Hundreds of thousands of Israeli Jewish settlers enjoy the privileges of citizens living within Israel proper, while Palestinians do not have citizenship status or civil rights and instead live under Israeli military law. Israeli punitive demolitions of Palestinian homes, while illegal under international law, persist with impunity. Furthermore, deeply imbricated in daily Palestinian life under occupation is the Israeli prison system.[55] Abraham argues, "These represent biotechnical interventions aiming to control and debilitate not only Palestinian bodies but also expressions of the Palestinian political will" ("Steven Salaita's" 74). This context for understanding the subjection and erasure of Palestinian lives emerged before the start of Israeli occupation in 1967. As I discussed in chapter one, from 1947–1949, approximately 700,000–800,000 Palestinians fled or were expelled from their homes, and between 400–600 Palestinian villages were destroyed by Zionist forces. The Nakba (catastrophe) is not a contained historical event of displacement, but rather a perpetual cycle of detention, dispossession, and death that continues unabated. Whereas Jewish Americans can visit and move to Israel freely, Palestinians in the Palestinian diaspora cannot (see fig. 4).

---

[55] In their 2018 Annual Violations Report, Addameer, a human rights NGO for Palestinian prisoners, states: "In 2018, the Israeli occupation forces (IOF) arrested around (6500) Palestinians, including (1080) children, (133) women, (6) PLC members and (17) journalists. Additionally, they issued (912) administrative detention orders, (398) of which were new." Military law in the occupied West Bank allows for the arrest of Palestinians without charge or warrant, which can lead to indefinite detention in prison. While some Palestinian detainees are charged, it is oftentimes not until months after their arrest, and some are never charged at all.

Fig. 4. Infographic from the historic Human Rights Watch report "A Threshold Crossed," released 27 April 2021, https://www.hrw.org/report/2021/04/27/threshold-crossed-israeli-authorities-and-crimes-apartheid-and-persecution.

As just one example of the risks entailed in speaking out in support of Palestinian rights, Zaiman earned herself a full profile on the blacklisting site Canary Mission (see figs. 5 and 6), a site which claims to document anti-Jewish and anti-Israel hatred (conflating criticism of Israel with antisemitism) but in actuality functions as a McCarthyist project that publicizes accusations of political disloyalty in order to suppress opposition. About the Canary Mission, Palestine Legal explains:

> As of January 2019, the site had profiles of 1,853 individuals and 563 professors. **Canary Mission targets Arab and Muslim students and faculty in particular**. Blacklisted individuals have reported being questioned by employers, graduate schools, and the FBI about their support for Palestinian rights after Canary Mission reached out. They have been put on leave, been denied bank accounts, and received death threats.
>
> **Canary Mission has also been used in the context of border enforcement and administration by Israeli officials** to question and deny entry to Israel and occupied Palestinian territory. Palestinians returning home, students, and faculty have reported seeing print-outs of their Canary Mission profiles when passing through Israeli border control and being questioned about content on those profiles. As documented in our 2018 Year-in-Review, Palestine Legal received several reports of Israeli security officials relying on the blacklisting site Canary Mission during airport screening. […]
> Fears of losing or not being able to secure a job, being targeted by law enforcement, prevented from visiting relatives in Palestine, or facing the threats and harassment that stem from being blacklisted have led some to abstain from engaging publicly in advocacy or support for Palestinian rights. In short, **this kind of online harassment results in significant chilling of human rights advocacy in the U.S. (original emphasis)**

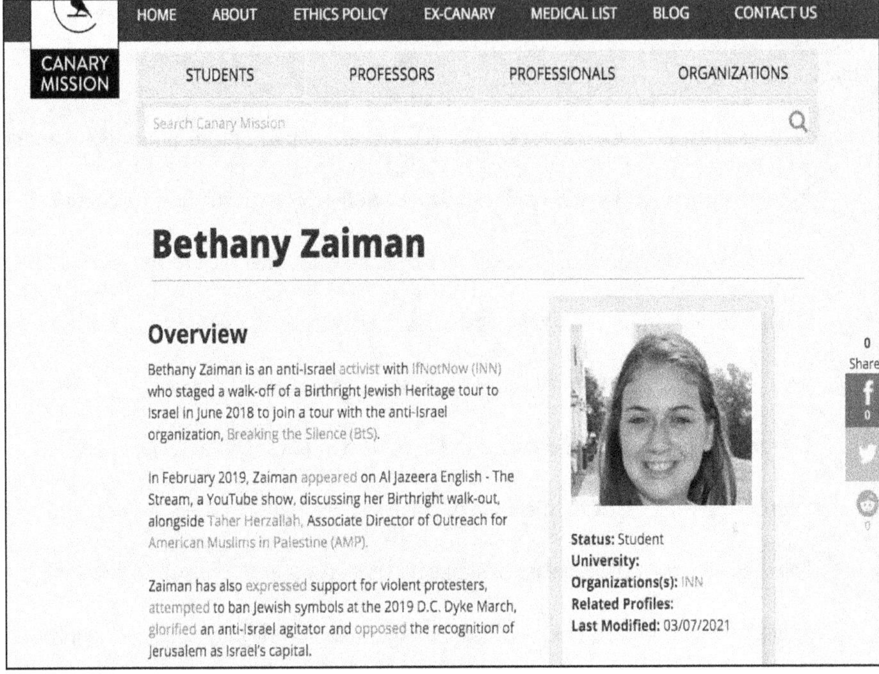

Fig. 5. Screenshot of the Canary Mission profile of Bethany Zaiman (screenshot: Brooke Hotez).

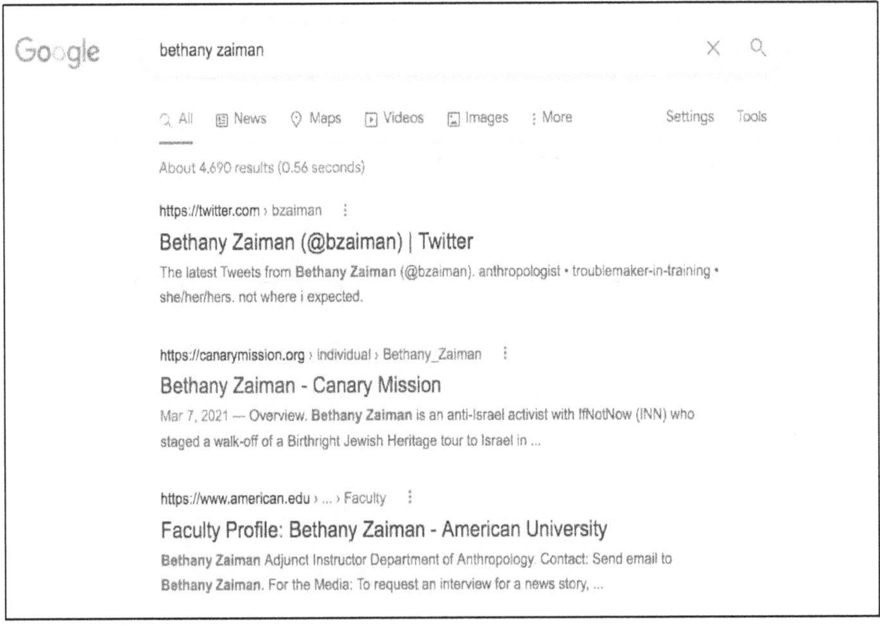

Fig. 6. In a Google search, the Canary Mission profile comes before her faculty profile (screenshot: Hotez).

#NotJustAFreeTrip by the group IfNotNow refuses the erasure of Palestinian life and history by dominant Zionist ideology through multiple protest strategies. The campaign aims to transform the ten-day trip's educational itinerary from within by directly engaging with Birthright. IfNotNow is a Jewish American anti-occupation organization founded in 2014 after Israel undertook Operation Protective Edge in Gaza. They have four key demands: that Birthright (1) mark the West Bank on every map, (2) educate participants on the daily nightmare of occupation, (3) show a military checkpoint from a Palestinian perspective, and (4) bring trips to Hebron to see what the policies of occupation have done to the city ("Confront"). To date, Birthright has not met these demands. Regardless, IfNotNow pushes for direct negotiations about Birthright's itinerary in an effort to normalize dialogue about Palestinian rights in the Jewish community. Subsequent walk-off actions have garnered prominent media coverage in *Los Angeles Times* (Parvini), *Haaretz* (JTA and Sales), *The Forward* (Pink), and *The Jerusalem Post* (Sharon), and elicited a front-page story in the *The New York Times* (Stockman). As a dissociative move to incorporate Palestinian perspectives in Jewish self-understanding about Israel, the four demands distinguish between appearance and reality and make an appeal to see the situation at hand in a different way.

In the refusal of Birthright's curriculum, #NotJustAFreeTrip's four demands enact a "dissociation of procedure" that re-names the situation in other terms (Schilb 39). Rhetorical refusals can work to expose exclusionary assumptions of the real by dominant ideologies. According to Schilb's framework, refusals occur when the author or speaker deliberately breaks the accepted protocol held by the audience in an appeal to higher principles (4–5). #NotJustAFreeTrip argues that the Birthright curriculum denies the existence of the Israeli occupation by failing to demarcate the West Bank on the tour's maps, excluding Palestinian voices from the trip, and not visiting Palestinian cities in the West Bank so that participants can see the occupation for themselves. Because Birthright has the stated mission of fostering Jewish identity and relationships with Israel, its trips have become highly regarded as a coming-of-age experience. Thus, the refusal to stay on this sacrosanct trip as a way to call for change could indeed be seen as defying the expectations of Zionist conceptions of the real.

In Fernheimer's case study, the State of Israel agreed to accept Black Hebrew Israelites as Jewish citizens through the Law of Return if they agreed to go through *halachic* conversion (which they declined). Although the Black Hebrew Israelites utilized dissociative techniques to expand the notion of Jewishness, this expanded definition was not accepted into "an already established tradition endowed with institutional power and authority" (63). Thus, while dissociation can reframe conceptions of reality in powerful ways from the perspective of a particular audience, dissociation can also lead to gridlock when institutional powers do not accept this break in terms. However, for Fernheimer, "Dissociative disruption allows for rhetorical moves to be successful simply by bringing about an awareness of alternative conceptions, even if these conceptions are not immediately embraced by those endowed with hegemonic and institutional power" (64). Dissociative disruption is, in short, a nonviolent strategy for engendering dialogue about an issue that has been ignored or silenced by dominant discourses and institutional authority. Thus, the #NotJustAFreeTrip activists' reinvented universal audience—even if not immediately accepted by institutional powers such as Taglit-Birthright—presents an awareness of alternative options for moving forward. It serves as a precursor or foundation for the possible conditions of future deliberation.

Taglit-Birthright has not yet complied with #NotJustAFreeTrip's four demands, but J Street, another prominent Jewish organization, has heeded the group's call. J Street is an American lobby organization that advocates for a two-state solution. It was founded in 2007 and has grown substantially in size and influence over the years. Although mainstream American liberals have supported a two-state solution since the 1990s, they have done so within a framework that fails to account for the asymmetrical power relations represented by, among other things, Palestinian disenfranchisement under Israeli martial law. J Street's recent program, the "Let My People Know Trip," reflects a shift in this mainstream discourse—it both describes the occupation as unjust and calls attention to the role of exclusionary Zionist narratives in perpetuating the conflict. The program's sign-up form reads: "The omission and erasure of Palestinian perspectives and narratives on Birthright trips create a political environment that allows home demolitions, settlement expansion, and other destructive policies of occupation to continue unchallenged" ("The Let My People Know Trip"). Building on #NotJustAFreeTrip's four demands, J Street's inaugural ten-day tour in July 2019 took participants into the West Bank from Hebron to Ramallah, met with Palestinian and Israeli peace activists, and critically reflected on the history of Zionism.

Rhetorical Memory in Alyssa's Open Letter

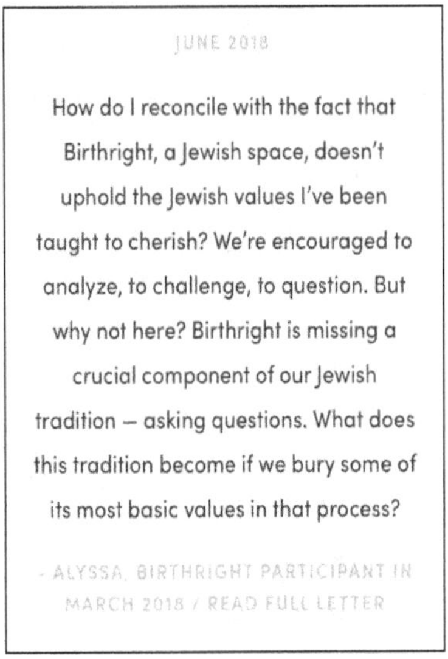

JUNE 2018

How do I reconcile with the fact that Birthright, a Jewish space, doesn't uphold the Jewish values I've been taught to cherish? We're encouraged to analyze, to challenge, to question. But why not here? Birthright is missing a crucial component of our Jewish tradition — asking questions. What does this tradition become if we bury some of its most basic values in that process?

– ALYSSA, BIRTHRIGHT PARTICIPANT IN MARCH 2018 / READ FULL LETTER

Fig. 7. Screenshot of #NotJustAFreeTrip media (screenshot: Hotez).

In addition to the four demands, the #NotJustAFreeTrip campaign offers a "Liberation Syllabus" as an alternative to Birthright's curriculum. The syllabus begins with Alyssa's open letter, "Dear Birthright Participant" (see fig. 7). In the tradition of Hertzberg, Alyssa's "Dear Birthright Participant" open letter discloses deeply felt personal experience to address an issue that is larger than the self, but through which the self's identity becomes constituted. Alyssa reflects on her Birthright experience at Yad Vashem, the Holocaust memorial museum in Jerusalem, and asks the question that haunts dominant Zionist rhetorical memory: Who occupied this land before us?

There's this point at the very end, after you've wound your way through the museum and thought about fear, hatred, love, how your family did or didn't make it … and you walk out and see this incredible landscape with a big open sky, and maybe you feel hopeful, or sad, or even grateful. I felt all of those things, and so I cried. […] But then I thought,

"Who lived here before? The land is so beautiful, how could it have been empty before?"

(Alyssa)

As I discussed in the rhetorical genealogy of Zionism's Third Persona in chapter one, in the early twentieth century, dominant Zionist ideology portrayed the land of Palestine as empty and barren. Despite the fact that a significant indigenous Arab majority already resided on and connected to the land in Palestine, "A land without a people for a people without a land" was a common Zionist slogan, along with "make the desert bloom." By portraying the land as barren and empty as its premise, the slogans in effect motivated Zionist colonization and justified the consequent dispossession of Palestinian *fellahin* (the peasant class). Put another way, the indigenous Arab population was not seen as civilized or fully human (depicted as nomadic and illiterate) and thus blended into the landscape itself as an obstacle to overcome. Although widely discredited by historians, today the myth of "A land without a people for a people without a land" permeates the dominant Zionist rhetorical memory in programs such as Birthright.

#NotJustAFreeTrip deploys multiple strategies to intervene in the dominant discourse. On the one hand, the group calls for concrete change with its four demands; on the other hand, it challenges the dominant Zionist worldview by addressing coexistent traumatic memories. Alyssa's disruptive statement, "how could it have been empty before?" destabilizes the singular ethnonationalist narrative. The results of this disruptive act cannot be predicted in advance. What happens, for instance, when the collective traumatic memories of the Holocaust and the Nakba are publicly deliberated together in the context of asymmetrical Palestinian-Israeli power relations? Political scientist Bashir Bashir and historian Amos Goldberg draw upon the notion of empathic unsettlement to get "at the core of [their] suggested new historical grammar and syntax" for the Holocaust and the Nakba (25). They contend that, unlike complete identification, which either appropriates the otherness of the Other into the sameness of the Self or further alienates and marginalizes the Other, empathic unsettlement operates in the "twilight zone" between the opposing spheres of appropriation and negation and disrupts the homogeneous finality sought by ethnonationalist frameworks (24). Thus, we can frame Alyssa's utterance— "Who lived here before?"—at Yad Vashem as empathically unsettling the insular Birthright itinerary.

Hebrew literature scholar Nurith Gertz asks, "Why are compassion and recognition of the Palestinian plight perceived by the Israeli public as a threat to the legitimacy of the State of Israel and to its very existence?" (161). Given that the Holocaust and the Nakba underlie Jewish and Palestinian nationalist claims to justice in similar yet different ways, Bashir and Goldberg argue that each side's empathic recognition of the other's trauma need not be interpreted as a threat to each other's claims (21). The perception of such a threat, in this argument, represents a false choice produced by the "pro-Israel versus pro-Palestinian" dichotomy. In the new grammar proposed by Bashir and Goldberg, these parallel (but not analogous) collective traumas can be deliberated together. In this light, empathic unsettlement can work toward a binational public deliberation of rhetorical memory as a form of decolonization that reimagines "Arab-Jewish democratic joint dwelling" (28). The "twilight zone" of empathetic unsettlement both recognizes the humanity of the Other and honors the Other's unique difference.

Alyssa enacts empathic unsettlement as a form of dissociation to jointly deliberate traumatic memory. In her letter, she writes:

Later, I asked my tour guide about the land around Yad Vashem. "It was nothing before," he told me, "just swamp." Just swamp. … I later looked up the history of lands near Yad Vashem and read reports that not too far away was once a Palestinian Arab village where, in 1948, over 100 villagers were killed. *Why couldn't my group talk about this other history as well?* (Alyssa, *emphasis added*)

The last line here attempts to hold Birthright's ethnonationalist curriculum accountable for the narrative erasure of Palestinian history. Alyssa also refuses the euphemism "just swamp" to describe an empty Palestine for Zionist settlement in her acknowledgment of the Nakba. Although #NotJustAFreeTrip does not take an official stance on Palestinians' right of return, Alyssa's empathic disruption can be read as laying the ground for rethinking binational memory by reflecting upon the 1948 destruction of Palestinian villages while at the Yad Vashem museum. In this context, Alyssa's questions are not mere questions; they evoke Palestinian trauma *alongside* Jewish trauma, and her refusal of the euphemistic erasure of Palestinian history exposes the Zionist commitment to covering up the underlying violence of its mythic origin story. Although Alyssa conjures up the Nakba alongside the Holocaust, she does so without explicitly naming it or calling attention to Palestinian refugees' right of return, which is commonly associated with the Nakba. As such, #NotJustAFreeTrip strategically pushes the boundaries of permissible political speech, which is governed by Jewish ethnonationalist conceptions of the real.

IfNotNow's #NotJustAFreeTrip campaign does not take an official stance on Palestinians' right of return, and its activists specifically focus on the occupation of the West Bank in their four demands. In this way, #NotJustAFreeTrip can be interpreted as supporting a two-state solution—a widely accepted platform among "pro-Israel, pro-peace" groups who also seek to end the occupation. IfNotNow activists speak as insiders who are attempting to both redefine the universal Jewish audience in anti-occupation terms and gain recognition for acceptable speech by implicitly appealing to a two-state solution. IfNotNow's lack of an explicit stance on Palestinians' right of return does not indicate that the group does not support this idea—indeed, Alyssa's open letter connects the Holocaust with the fate of Palestinians in the Nakba, a reference that is typically tied to right of return. By not taking an explicit stance, however, IfNotNow strategically positions themselves in relation to ethnonationalist conceptions of the universal Jewish audience in order to disrupt dominant narratives from within. As such, IfNotNow's rhetorical refusal to remain silent about the occupation also embodies a refusal to be dismissed as "no more than a particular audience" (Perelman and Olbrechts-Tyteca 34).

#ReturnTheBirthright and Anti-Zionism

Fig. 8. Screenshot of JVP Instagram post of activists and friends Ghada Karmi and Ellen Siegel (screenshot: Hotez).

Whereas IfNotNow's focus on the occupied West Bank can be read within the permissible framework of a two-state solution, Jewish Voice for Peace's #ReturnTheBirthright crosses the boundaries of that permissibility by explicitly supporting the Palestinians' right of return. Jewish Voice for Peace (JVP) is a nonprofit organization with 18,000 members that was founded in 1996 by three Jewish women who "realized they could no longer keep silent about Israel's occupation" ("Mission"). JVP's overall rhetorical aim is to challenge the Zionist formulation of Jewish privilege in Israel's Law of Return by contrasting it with Palestinians' right of return (see fig. 8). The campaign also employs dissociative contrast to highlight other inequities between Jews and Palestinians in Israel and Palestine, such as differences in each groups' freedom of movement, certain lives' heightened grievability, and certain voices' permission to narrate over others.

The #ReturnTheBirthright manifesto openly discusses the Nakba, which is given crucial consideration in the campaign's rhetorical refusal of birthright. The manifesto states: "Today, when young Jews are taken by Birthright guides on hikes through forests in Israel, they still sometimes stumble across the remnants of these destroyed Palestinian villages [from 1948], covered over, often deliberately, by the Jewish National Fund's tree-planting programs" ("Young Jews"). The manifesto contrasts that which is visible with that which is hidden in order to reframe Zionist value hierarchies. This contrast also highlights the Jewish National Fund's (JNF) tree-planting program in Zionist policies of Palestinian erasure that disavow the JNF's complicity in covering over the destruction of Palestinian villages.

The ethnonationalist notion of Jewish birthright is not just legally codified through Israel's Law of Return — it is bound up with the logic that Palestinians represent a demographic and existential threat to Israel. The #ReturnTheBirthright manifesto challenges this logic by breaking the links that define Jewish birthright in exclusionary terms. It states: "Taking a

Birthright trip today means playing an active role in helping the state promote Jewish 'return'

while rejecting the Palestinian right of return. … And as we reject [the Birthright trip], we

commit to promoting the right to return of Palestinian refugees" ("Young Jews"). As I discussed

in chapter two, from a dominant Zionist perspective, the Palestinian people are a demographic

threat[56] insofar as Palestinian Arabs will outnumber Israeli Jews especially if Palestinian

refugees[57] are allowed to return to their homeland under international law.[58] This defines Israel's

Jewish character by the size of its population and, therefore, sees Palestinians' existence within

"Greater Israel" as an inherent danger to the state's character and right to exist. However, for

Palestinians, their right of return is not motivated by hatred for Israel as a Jewish state but by a

political demand for justice and restitution. Bawarshi argues, "This longing to return home

persists to this day and is a constant presence in Palestinian discourse" ("Discourse" 9). In this

sense, #ReturnTheBirthright upends the exclusionary logic of ethnonationalism and reconstitutes

Jewish survival as interdependent with, rather than opposed to, Palestinian rights.

---

[56] The notion of a Palestinian demographic threat in Zionist discourse can be traced back to the origins of the movement under the euphemism of "population transfer." Zionists believed in the Hebrew conquest of labor and land, a vision that included only Jews and excluded native Arab inhabitants. In the first half of the twentieth century, dominant Zionist ideologues such as Theodor Herzl, Chaim Weizmann, Vladimir Jabotinsky, and David Ben-Gurion justified what they variously called compulsory transfer, resettlement, and population exchange through the colonialist belief that Palestine's native Arab majority was a nomadic and uncivilized population with no sense of nationhood or legitimate attachment to the land.

[57] The United Nations Relief and Works Agency (UNRWA) defines Palestine refugees as "persons whose normal place of residence was Palestine during the period from 1 June 1946 to 15 May 1948, and who lost both home and means of livelihood as a result of the 1948 conflict." The UNRWA website states: "When the Agency began operations in 1950, it was responding to the needs of about 750,000 Palestine refugees. Today, some 5 million Palestine refugees are eligible for UNRWA services" ("Palestine"). Since 1948, and again in 1967, Palestinian refugees in the West Bank, Gaza Strip, Jordan, and Lebanon have been stateless and lack the right to vote for the governments that exercise control over them. For an excellent "Myth vs Reality" backgrounder about Palestinian refugees, see Alhamdan.

[58] For example, UN Resolution 194 (passed in 1948), which officially recognized Palestinians' right of return for the first time.

The authors of JVP's #ReturnTheBirthright Student Voices letter campaign consistently target this notion of Jewish versus non-Jewish birthright to the land. Five out of the seven letters are authored by students who self-identify as Jews, and the other two are authored by Palestinian students who speak out about how they feel seeing their Jewish peers take free 10-day trips to Israel. The letters utilize testimonial and contrast to highlight the one-dimensional nature of Birthright's educational narrative. Daniel Kaplan's testimonial reflects on the fact that Palestinians are a "significant proportion of the population directly and indirectly governed by Israel, yet [they] are mostly erased in Birthright's framing of Israel." Julia Wedgle uses the mundane metaphor of the "E-ZPass" tollbooth to contrast Jews' and Palestinians' freedom of movement in the West Bank:

> To get to Jerusalem from the illegal settlement, we had to pass through a checkpoint. We were told it was a tollbooth. When I asked why we did not pay the toll, I was told we had an E-ZPass. We did in fact have an E-ZPass, but not like the one we have on cars in Boston. Instead, it was our Jewish privilege, embodied by the Taglit-Birthright Israel sign on the front of our bus. As Jewish tourists, we passed right through the checkpoint, while Palestinians attempting to cross it to get to work or to the hospital were stuck in multiple-hour-long queues. In five years, 67 Palestinian babies were born at checkpoints. 36 of them died. That doesn't happen at tollbooths. (Wedgle and Carter)

Here, the E-ZPass highlights the contrast between the Jews' freedom of movement and the Israeli state's control over the Palestinians' freedom of movement. Whereas the checkpoint functions as a tollbooth for Jews, who pay the toll with their Jewish birthright, for Palestinians it functions as a true military checkpoint and often becomes a matter of life and death.

Wedgle's letter encourages her readers, Birthright participants, to question both the trip Birthright and the notion of Jewish birthright to Israel. This is similar to how Perelman and Olbrechts-Tyteca argue that audiences "pass judgment on one another" (35), and how Schilb argues that rhetorical refusals invite the target audience to accept the speaker's break in norms and become a reinvented audience that then passes judgment on its previously accepted protocol (39). Schilb contends that "[s]uccess, in this respect, would mean that members of that audience now criticize the audience they used to be" (95). Wedgle reconstructs the exclusionary logic of ethnonationalist birthright by framing her piece in terms of the Jewish tradition of justice within which she was raised. After establishing this appeal, she argues that her participation in a Birthright trip molded her into a Palestine solidarity activist:

> "Tzedek, Tzedek, Tirdof: Justice Justice, you shall pursue" were the words I was taught to live by growing up as a Jewish-American [*sic*]. I was also taught I had a "Birthright" to Israel—that I should connect to, travel to and even live there, simply because I am Jewish. My Birthright trip and the two months I spent in Israel/Palestine afterward transformed me into the anti-Zionist Jewish woman I am today. Somehow I saw through Birthright's propaganda and learned to apply my Jewish values to all people, especially those oppressed in my name. (Wedgle and Carter)

Framing her experience within the Jewish tradition, Wedgle employs the E-ZPass metaphor to provide contrast and highlight the injustice of non-Jewish discrimination in Israel and Palestine. This dissociative move breaks the links in underlying norms—for example, the idea that Israel can be both a Jewish *and* a democratic state when, in fact, it is a democracy for Jews, an ethnocracy in which the state apparatus is controlled by the dominant group to further its own interests at the expense of others. Many American Jews hold tight to the idea that Israel can be both a democratic and a Jewish state; Wedgle rejects this notion and recalibrates the assumed

value hierarchy to expose a different reality to her audience. If her efforts are successful, her

audience will question the Birthright organization and the concept of Jewish birthright to Israel,

and then pass judgment on its previous out-of-hand acceptance of both the organization and the

concept. Wedgle refuses the euphemistic language of the "tollbooth" and insists on both seeing

and revealing the military checkpoint for what it is. Through this act of refusal, Wedgle reinvents

the universal Jewish audience as a definitional concept of identity in relation to Palestine

solidarity and activism.

As mentioned above, two of the #ReturnTheBirthright Student Voices campaign's seven

letters are authored by Palestinian students. In this way, JVP places itself at the forefront of

Palestine solidarity activism by co-articulating a shared, critical, self-reflexive sense of

belonging. Self-reflexivity entails reflecting on one's own privilege, power, and positionality

within systems of domination and exploitation. In this regard, a co-articulation of belonging

across different communities does not assume an underlying evenness—rather, it reflects on the

responsibility that those who hold power and privilege must dismantle structural inequalities.

Butler questions the relation between acts by individuals and the conditions of possibility that

give rise to those acts: "We are at once acted upon and acting, and our 'responsibility' lies in the

juncture between the two. What can I do with the conditions that form me? What do they

constrain me to do? What can I do to transform them?" (*Precarious* 16). Butler highlights the

role of reflection on one's positionality to enact strategic transformation. #ReturnTheBirthright

authors practice critical self-reflexivity by centering Palestinian dispossession as their ethical

starting point and by incorporating actual Palestinian voices into the campaign. This constitutes a

radical re-envisioning of the universal Jewish audience.

In addition to potential dismissal as a particular audience, #ReturnTheBirthright activists

risk being labeled as antisemites or terrorist sympathizers. In context, these labels imply that

Jewish dissenters are self-hating traitors of their people.[59] JVP's avowed anti-Zionism and

support of the Palestinian right of return have made it the target of many mainstream Jewish

groups' and publications' disapproval and condemnation, including the Anti-Defamation League

(ADL) and *Commentary*,[60] a monthly magazine founded in 1945 by the American Jewish

Committee. The ADL is a major nonprofit organization established in 1913 to fight antisemitism

and other forms of bigotry, and the mainstream Jewish community looks to the ADL as a type of

moral compass with regard to the rising tides of antisemitism. The ADL also tracks what it sees

as anti-Israel animus and often applies the "3D Test" framework, conflating dissenting views of

Israel with antisemitism. Many Israel advocates employ the "3D Test," which argues that when

Zionism is deemed a form of racism Israel is being demonized, delegitimized, and held to a

double standard (Sharansky). The implicit attitude underlying this premise is that the State of

Israel stands for all Jewish people. Such interpretations conflate Palestinian rights activism with

anti-Israel animus and antisemitism, deflect the substance of claims from Palestinian

perspectives, and stifle dissent by "weaponizing" charges of antisemitism.[61]

Thus, the ADL sees political speech that it perceives as challenging Israel's right to exist

(a form of delegitimization) as antisemitic. The ADL has an entire online report about JVP,

which it describes as a "radical anti-Israel activist group" with "extreme views" that "demonize

---

[59] The Anti-Defamation League's report about JVP insinuates as such. The report states that JVP is "dismissive of Israeli fears of terrorism perpetrated by Palestinians, and comes dangerously close to excusing Palestinian violence against Israelis" ("Jewish Voice"). In Israel, Palestinian human rights defenders are often explicitly accused of being terrorist apologists and traitors to the Jewish people. See Sfard, "Israel's Human Rights Activists Aren't Traitors" in *The New York Times* about incitement against human rights activists in the Knesset.

[60] See Muravchik, "Not So Jewish, Not For Peace: How Jewish Voice for Peace falsifies Judaism and glorifies terrorism. A deep dive" in *Commentary* from April 2019.

[61] Some blaming of Israel does perpetuate antisemitic conspiracies and stereotypes. However, this dissertation focuses on how charges of antisemitism are weaponized to chill dissent. See footnote 48.

Israel" ("Jewish Voice"). In this report, the ADL argues that "radical expressions of Anti-Zionism can be motivated by anti-Semitism, and can perpetuate anti-Semitic stereotypes" ("Jewish Voice"). The ADL references the #ReturnTheBirthright campaign as evidence of JVP's "ideologically extreme approach to Israel and Zionism," and, by inference, antisemitism ("Jewish Voice"). Nonetheless, the #ReturnTheBirthright student activists take an anti-Zionist stance by grappling with Zionist ideology from a Palestinian perspective. From this perspective, being a Zionist or accepting Zionism is absurd—doing so entails accepting the subordination of the Palestinians. Much of Palestinian politics with regard to Israel is therefore read as hostile, extreme, and antisemitic by the dominant Zionist discourse. The ADL's use of the "3D Test," for instance, forecloses the possibility of Palestinian self-determination by charging the speaker with antisemitism, thereby painting the Palestinian people as an existential threat to Israel. This discourse's logic of the demographic threat, in particular, sees Palestinians' mere existence as a challenge to Israel's "right to exist"—in other words, they see all expressions of Palestinians' right of return as delegitimizing and therefore threatening to the State of Israel.

In 2014, six anonymous Palestinian students affiliated with #ReturnTheBirthright's Student Voices campaign co-authored an editorial in *The Tufts Daily* titled, "Those without a Birthright." In the editorial, they expressed their sadness that, while their fellow Jewish students could go on a Birthright trip, they themselves were not able to visit the land from which many of their grandparents were expelled in 1948:

> Kind reader, understand that our hearts ache when we see photographs of friends and acquaintances swimming in the sea our grandparents once swam in. Our hearts ache when we see photographs of classmates posing in front of the mosques and churches our grandparents once prayed in, but now pray to one day see. Our hearts ache when we see

pictures of peers eating the fruits of the land we have grown up hearing of, but never

tasted. Our hearts ache when we see our classmates posing next to exotic camels and

mysterious Bedouins in a grotesque charade of our culture. Our hearts ache each time we

are reminded that we do not share this birthright. ("Those without a Birthright")

In this piece, repetition of the phrase "our hearts ache" conveys a sense of culminating emotional

weight. Such repetition also communicates the authors' overwhelming sense that they cannot

escape or look away from the dual absence and presence of their homeland, as a new photo may

suddenly appear on a social media feed or around campus.

#ReturnTheBirthright student activists take an anti-Zionist stance and grapple with the

ideology from the perspective of Palestinians. As seen in the ADL's report on JVP, the dominant

frame views anti-Zionism as an ideologically extreme position that can be antisemitic in intent

and effect. The Palestinian political position with regard to Israel is necessarily anti-Zionist. For

Palestinians, to be a Zionist or to accept Zionism is an absurdity that would mean accepting their

subordination. In the dominant U.S.-Israel frame, the "new antisemitism" of anti-Zionism then

renders much of Palestinian politics in terms of hostility and extremism. This interpretive

framework of antisemitism and anti-Zionism has its own effect: to not only divert consideration

of the claims at hand, but to also charge the author or speaker of complicity in perpetuating

antisemitic stereotypes. The effect is to foreclose the intelligibility of Palestinian self-

determination. In other words, the Palestinian people come to embody the existential threat to

Israel as both a security threat (as terrorists) and a demographic threat. Particularly through the

logic of demographic threat, Palestinians therefore challenge Israel's "right to exist" by virtue of

their existence as a people. They come to embody the anti-Israel delegitimization aspect of the

"3D Test," and as such are always already presumed to be antisemitic especially when

Palestinians claim their right to return. In "Permission to Narrate," Said writes about the "disciplinary communications apparatus" that works to suppress Palestinian viewpoints and criticism of Israel (30). In this apparatus, discourse on terrorism can also function as a veil of negation that prevents the possibility of a humanizing Palestinian narrative. Said's essay attests to the "wilderness of mirrors" of dominating Zionist frames and anti-Arab stereotypes that Palestinians must navigate in order to assert their first-person narratives of identity (37).

The anonymous Palestinian American student co-authors take the risk of navigating the wilderness of mirrors by being emotionally vulnerable in expressing their own suffering and that of their families and communities to the dominant group: "We are writing to you, the curious, compassionate and questioning Tufts student. We hope that our words resonate with you and form a deeper understanding of what it means to be Palestinian on this campus" ("Those without a Birthright"). They attempt to push through the Zionist logic of existential threat in their search for communicable self-understanding. They do this in part by appealing to goodwill and a higher moral ground. Through the metaphor of a photograph, they contrast Jews' and Palestinians' experiences on two levels. First, as Palestinians, they are not permitted to travel to Palestine like their Jewish counterparts. Second, the co-authors contrast Jewish and Palestinian students' affective reaction to the same set of photographs: "For you, these events may be innocuous, exotic and enjoyable. For us, your photos create a feeling we hope no one will ever have to endure, no matter where they are from. We feel the weight of our lives that could have been, but never were" ("Those without a Birthright"). Palestinian life and loss are not worth grieving in the dominant Zionist framework (Butler, *Precarious* 32–36). #ReturnTheBirthright reimagines the ethnonationalist definition of the universal Jewish audience by acknowledging Palestinian loss and incorporating a critique of Zionism from the perspective of its victims.

Who is the Rhetorical Audience for JVP?

JVP is both a formidable part of the organized American Jewish community while shunned from it for being an avowedly anti-Zionist Jewish organization that supports BDS[62] and Palestinian right of return. Early in 2019, JVP released an official statement declaring itself "unequivocally" opposed to Zionism. This statement ignited discussion in the larger U.S. Jewish community and internally among JVP members. The constructive response among anti-Zionist and liberal Zionist American Jews debates the significance of the statement and to whom it is or is not addressed.

The JVP statement titled, "Our Approach to Zionism," opens with the clause: "Jewish Voice for Peace is guided by a vision of justice, equality and freedom for all people. We unequivocally oppose Zionism because it is counter to those ideals." The statement, about 600 words, depicts Zionism from the perspective of Palestinian dispossession. In this regard, the statement is fundamentally one of solidarity with "Palestinians fighting for their own liberation" ("Our Approach"). Is JVP addressing a Jewish audience, the Palestinian people, or both? JVP member Rabbi Michael Davis argues that the statement is "inward-looking" and fails to address

---

[62] The Boycott, Divestment, and Sanctions (BDS) movement formed in 2005 and is a call from Palestinian civil society for nonviolent resistance against Israeli apartheid and colonialism. The campaign has three demands for Israel: (1) ending its occupation and colonization of all Arab lands and dismantling the Wall (the separation barrier along the West Bank erected in 2004), (2) recognizing the fundamental rights of Arab-Palestinian citizens of Israel to full equality, and (3) respecting, protecting and promoting the rights of Palestinian refugees to return to their homes and properties as stipulated in UN Resolution 194 ("What").

BDS and Palestinian right of return remain red lines in the mainstream U.S. Jewish community. The dominant pro-Israel worldview frames BDS and right of return as existential threats to the State of Israel. For one, in this Holocaust-centered Israeli security frame, BDS is charged with antisemitism because it is linked to boycott of Jewish businesses during Nazi Germany (see Nasr and Alkousaa). U.S.-Israel anti-BDS discourse also accuses the BDS movement of anti-Jewish animus for "singling out" Israel for boycott presumably by virtue of the fact that it is a *Jewish* state (see "Bigotry, Discrimination, Anti-Semitism" by the Israeli American Council for an example of the way the dominant U.S.-Israeli worldview defames the BDS movement with antisemitism accusations).

Critics of anti-BDS discourse not only point out First Amendment rights regarding free speech and boycott but also argue that charges of "singling out" Israel are part of a larger "whataboutism" rhetorical strategy that distracts from the substance of the issue at hand (see Hasan and Sayedahmed). Moreover, critics of anti-BDS argue that BDS supporters are responding to a legitimate solidarity call from Palestinian society in the struggle for freedom.

either a Palestinian or Jewish audience, and instead addresses itself, self-identified anti-Zionist

Jews. In the statement, JVP describes Israel as a settler colonial apartheid state; Zionism is "a

political ideology founded on erasure" ("Our Approach"). The statement acknowledges the range

of views in the history of Zionism but remains focused on the dominant strain that has

manifested the century-long war.

Jewish Currents published a roundtable of five contributors in response to JVP's anti-

Zionist stance. In her roundtable piece, feminist and ethnic studies scholar Manijeh Nasrabadi

incorporates first-person narrative to reflect on what the statement says about Jewishness and

identification with anti-Zionism. She reflects on growing up in an anti-Zionist household with

her father, a Zoroastrian immigrant from Iran, and her mother, an Ashkenazi Jew from New

Jersey. Growing up as an anti-Zionist Iranian Jew, Nasrabadi writes that it was difficult to claim

her Jewish identity because she felt "ashamed of Jewish support for Zionism" and set apart from

Ashkenazi Jewish relatives and other families. The JVP statement and the deliberative, collective

writing process leading up to its final product "truly amazed" Nasrabadi. She writes, "I have seen

American Jews of my generation and younger, who have been brought up with Zionist

education, reckon openly with a history of Zionist crimes against Palestinians that once felt

impossible to acknowledge." In this way, JVP's statement works to authorize this reckoning as

an address to those who have been and felt alienated by Zionist rhetoric in the organized Jewish

community.

For Nasrabadi, the statement's process and final release open a space for reinvented

Jewishness that not only rejects apartheid and settler colonialism but also considers different

ways of facing antisemitism and historical trauma. She writes, "JVP's statement does not seek to

minimize the brutality of antisemitism or demand that Jews get over the past and move on;

instead the statement enacts a new kind of confrontation with antisemitic legacies and ongoing dangers." Nasrabadi argues that Jewish anti-Zionism and Palestine solidarity activism work to understand the history of anti-Jewish hatred in a decolonizing political imaginary that rejects Jewish statehood and military power as the only means for securing Jewish safety and continuity.

Butler contends that Zionist rhetoric of existential threat exposes itself, in that "Israel in its present form cannot do without its mechanisms of dispossession without destroying itself as Israel. In this sense, the threat to Israel is a consequence of its fundamental dependency on dispossession and expulsion for its existence" (*Parting* 214). Thus, any form of Zionism that believes in a Jewish majority and complete Jewish control of the land is morally untenable, by virtue of the fact that ethnocentric supremacy relies upon the continuing subjugation and minoritization of non-Jews in order to maintain itself as such. Is JVP working to respond to the demand of alterity? Butler—by way of Edward Said and Mahmoud Darwish—suggests this response is an impossible but necessary task. How can the demands from alterity become audible as something other than an existential threat to the hegemonic self? In other words, if JVP is addressing the organized Jewish community, the substance of the address is both inaudible and perceived as a threat.

In one sense, as I discussed in chapter three, Butler argues that heeding the demand of alterity entails a dissociation of Jewish self-identity from Zionist birthright insofar as it signifies exclusionary ethnonationalism and a Jewish majority in historic Palestine. Butler further advocates for an ethical relation to alterity as a way toward binationalism, not a two-state binational solution but a one-state binational political system and cultural coexistence. Binationalism and the shedding of settler colonial logic require recognition of parallel but not analogous histories of dispossession and dispersion. The State of Israel relies upon the opposite function of unremitting erasure of Palestinian history (Zionism's Third Persona), and through this effacement Israel perpetuates the Nakba, physically and discursively. Butler points to the Israeli criminalization of Palestinian Nakba Day (the day after Israeli Independence Day), and that "the question of publicly acknowledging the destruction and dispossession of Palestinians in 1948 is no merely symbolic matter; if anything, it is powerfully symbolic" (*Parting* 206).

Jewish anti-Zionism, conceptualized as decolonizing praxis in an ethical relation to Palestinian freedom, occasions a reinvention of Jewish identity, one that relinquishes Zionist interpretations of Jewish suffering (from Holocaust to renewal) and instead draws upon diasporic tradition as a way to reconstitute identity through the exilic, foreign Other of the self. Butler argues, "For Said, diasporic existence is constituted in the midst of cultural heterogeneity, negotiating difference, indeed affirming difference or plurality as a condition of its own existence" (*Parting* 215). In this way, Jewish diasporic tradition becomes a cultural resource for identification with the Other also in exile. As I discussed in chapter three, shared histories of dispossession and dispersion become the shared ground that both enable identification and identity's transformation. To welcome the stranger is to welcome the self; the Jewish self is the stranger, the wanderer, the refugee, as Palestinians have also become the wanderer and the refugee.

In her roundtable response, Nasrabadi writes, "The JVP statement asks Jews to make new meaning out of the losses we have suffered, to turn this suffering into the very lens that brings Palestinian suffering into focus. Only by linking the safety and flourishing of Palestinians and Jews … can we recover any hope of a peaceful, democratic future." In another roundtable piece, daughter of Nakba exiles and Palestinian historian Sherene Seikaly calls the JVP statement "brave, historic, and long overdue." Seikaly argues, "In 2019, white supremacy, settler-colonialism, and right-wing populism have triumphed. These triumphs leave no room for hesitation, whataboutism, and the tears of privilege. These triumphs render intersectional solidarity a matter not of choice but of survival. Antisemitism, Orientalism, anti-blackness, and Islamophobia are mutually constituted and linked phenomena." In Seikaly's response, the JVP statement is doing a different type of work in response to antisemitism and Jewish suffering that stands in contradistinction to Zionist interpretations of the same discriminatory phenomena. Instead of seeing insular barriers and militarized borders as a way to protect against anti-Jewish hatred, Seikaly argues that JVP's "Approach to Zionism" forges intersectional alliances and levies privileged Jewish support in the fight against race-based prejudice and violence.

Although JVP's statement addresses the fraught topic of Zionism from a Jewish perspective that centers Palestinian dispossession and as such enacts a modality of ethical relation though political solidarity, some key respondents and JVP members oppose taking an official stand on Zionism. An internal objection by JVP members titled "Unequivocally support Palestinian rights; avoid ideological labels" forwarded to the JVP Chapters Google Groups contends that the JVP anti-Zionism statement exacerbates the divide between JVP as an outsider organization in relation to the organized U.S. Jewish community. The internal objection argues that JVP needs to strategically redefine the universal Jewish audience in order to foster Jewish cultural transformation and normalize dialogue about Palestinian equal rights. By taking a stand as anti-Zionist, JVP in effect isolates itself apart from the mainstream community and further alienates those who may be sympathetic to Palestinian rights but feel that anti-Zionism is anti-Israel, equating to an existential threat of Jewish identity. The internal objection is endorsed by the Portland and Sacramento JVP chapters and signed by more than forty individual JVP members. They argue:

The adoption of anti-Zionism seems addressed mostly to current and potential JVP allies who already share our programmatic positions. While some may welcome the statement, we don't believe that maintaining and strengthening such alliances requires us to risk undermining efforts to draw in fellow Jewish Americans, who JVP has said – and we agree – are the main target of our base-building goals.

Because anti-Zionism is adamantly viewed as "the new antisemitism" in the American Jewish establishment and organized community, the internal opposition contends that the JVP anti-Zionism statement feeds into dominant logic rather than unraveling it; the statement perpetuates such diametrically opposed narratives that are locked in the hero/villain binary, rather than working to bridge frames. In his roundtable response, Davis is equally critical and agrees with the internal opposition that the anti-Zionism statement in effect reproduces the for-or-against impasse that the organization otherwise claims to depart from. He writes, "In issuing this statement on Zionism, JVP is drawing 'red lines' on others in our community that are so often applied to us, for the comfort of ideological purity on the left, and at the expense of our goal of Jewish communal transformation."

In the internal objection, co-signers seem to empathize with their former selves who once ascribed to a one-dimensional pro-Israel narrative mostly due to ignorance and not because of outright anti-Arab racism. They argue from a unique position that can understand Zionism as something other than settler colonialism as a type of national pride that is dear to Jewish identity, while at the same time recognizing Zionism as an inherently exclusionary political ideology that relies upon ethnic cleansing to maintain itself. They write, "Like many Americans, some of us were not fully aware of the ongoing Nakba and the complex history of Zionism before joining JVP. Recognizing this, JVP's prior openness to people with varying views regarding Zionism was invaluable for maintaining an open path leading to deeper and more accurate understanding of the stakes in Israel/Palestine" (Singer). The demand of alterity becomes audible through a nonlinear process of education, perhaps a jolting encounter, gradual awareness, and self-reflection. Butler, in part, is arguing for the revival of Jewish exilic tradition as a modality of ethical relation. This becomes at once the grounds for hearing the demand of alterity in its unsettling familiarity *and* a dispossession from that ground, a shared ground that is both familiar and alien, a rhetoric of defamiliarizing of the familiar.

The internal JVP objection urges further dialogue about the official statement on Zionism and its implications for effectively reconstituting the universal Jewish audience. But who does the vanguard speak to?[63] On the one hand, by taking an anti-Zionist stance in support of Palestinians' right of return, JVP can be dismissed as a particular audience that alienates those who may be sympathetic to Palestinian rights but feel that anti-Zionism is antisemitic. On the other hand, if JVP's refusal might be acknowledged as playing a vanguard role by leading the way toward a decolonized imaginary of belonging for both Palestinians and Israelis, as Abraham suggests, then reaching the mainstream U.S. Jewish audience is not the goal, but rather that Palestine solidarity vanguard activists are creating an audience anew. For instance, JVP uses dissociation to break the links that codify the Palestinians' right of return as a demographic existential threat to Jewish survival and reconfigures this value hierarchy in terms that redefine Jewish continuity as inextricably bound up with Palestinian rights.

The rhetorical refusal of birthright provides an example of how ethnonationalist ideologies shape universality in exclusionary terms and regulate the boundaries of permissible political speech. An examination of the campaigns, #NotJustAFreeTrip and

---

[63] See Abraham, "Chomsky's Audience Problem: Is Anyone Listening?"

#ReturnTheBirthright, brings to light the competing constructions of the universal audience and claims of the real. JVP's hashtag #ReturnTheBirthright enacts dissociative disruption in dominant discourse with the combination of "Return" and "Birthright." The hashtag performs a provocative refusal that can simultaneously mean "return the Birthright trip" and "return the Jewish birthright," where "Return" is also a reference to Israel's Law of Return. This is a rhetorical refusal in that they are not necessarily giving up Jewish birthright in terms of its theological significance; rather, by implicating Israel's Law of Return, the hashtag transforms the concept of birthright from an ethnonationalist prerogative to a value of justice for all.

By reinventing the universal Jewish audience with Palestinian voices, JVP envisions an altogether new universal audience that is currently taking shape. In this way, JVP activists remain at the forefront of imagining a binational rhetoric of belonging for both Israelis and Palestinians. IfNotNow's #NotJustAFreeTrip also demands the inclusion of Palestinian voices in the Birthright itinerary, and J Street has taken up the challenge of Palestinian representation in its programming and advocacy. IfNotNow's rhetorical refusal of the Birthright trip diverges from JVP's refusal of an exclusionary Jewish birthright to Israel. While J Street and IfNotNow operate within the two-state framework of acceptable speech, JVP exceeds that framework by advocating for the Palestinian right of return as a form of reparative criticism to address the injustice of the Nakba.

Chapter 5

Teaching Rhetorical Refusal in the Writing Classroom

The question of who constitutes the universal audience as a construct of a particular author or speaker becomes a political question enmeshed in fraught power relations of intersectional identity. In chapter four, I analyzed such political dimensions in the rhetorical refusal of birthright by young Jewish American activists. Through the rhetorical refusal, the activists reinvent the construct of the universal Jewish audience from the position of a particular audience. They reimagine the Zionist construct of the universal Jewish audience in a way that challenges underlying assumptions of exclusionary ethnonationalism and works to incorporate Palestinian rights and voices into the audience. One challenge is whether and how the hegemonic group that dominates definitions of the universal Jewish audience in the mainstream organized community responds to or accepts this reinvented formulation from the activists. It may be rejected or ignored. Nonetheless, through Fernheimer's theory of dissociative disruption, I show how the activists present an alternative conception of the universal audience, whether or not it is accepted by institutional authorities. This alternative conception can work to lay the grounds for conditions of possibility for future deliberation.

Like Fernheimer, Velasco revisits the Perelmanian concept of the universal audience to consider its usage for political critique. Velasco shows how the notion of universality can circulate in discursive networks to reinforce hegemonic power/knowledge relations. In a sense, Velasco is arguing that the universal audience is never apolitical, and that the hegemonic notion of universality as such works to depoliticize the political by naturalizing the status quo. It then *appears* to be apolitical through the naturalization of dominant ideology and mythos as the taken for granted reality. Velasco argues, "In this light, appealing to the universal audience can be seen as an argumentative strategy deeply ensconced in all forms of symbolic action, one which always attempts to universalize and naturalize as 'fact' or as 'truth' that which is local, historical and potentially partisan" (60–61). The universal audience is political because it constructs and advocates for conceptions of the real others. Regarding notions of the real, Perelman and Olbrechts-Tyteca argue, "Each individual, each culture, has thus its own conception of the universal audience. The study of these variations would be very instructive, as we would learn from it what men, at different times in history, have regarded as *real, true*, and *objectively valid*" (33, *original emphasis*). I am interested in the ways in which rhetorical refusals work to expose assumptions of the real by dominant ideologies, and how this framework can be utilized pedagogically.

In this chapter, I explore the way that teaching rhetorical refusal in the writing classroom can cultivate a critical rhetorical awareness in students, particularly when it comes to power relations and what rhetorician Nancy Welch calls "questions of audience discernment" (306). The subtitle in *Rhetorical Refusals: Defying Audiences' Expectations* by Schilb also points to analytical concerns regarding the audience question. As I discussed in chapter four, rhetorical refusals occur when the author or speaker deliberately breaks accepted protocol held by the audience in an appeal to higher moral ground. Schilb contends that refusals can "spark better reflection in their audiences than does the usual languages of politics" (178) and I look at how studying such rhetorical refusals can also spark reflection in students. Schilb stresses that rhetorical refusals "need to be judged case by case" (177). In and of themselves, as a strategy, rhetorical refusals are neither inherently good nor bad, effective nor ineffective. Thus, students can also learn about the significance of context by judging rhetorical refusal situations case by case.

As I demonstrated in chapter two, the Perelmanian approach indicates that audiences pass judgment on one another. In the instance of a rhetorical refusal, two different constructs of audience or "groups" are at work. The first group adheres to already accepted protocol according to the given discourse community, and in the break with protocol, refusers appeal to a second group, or to an imagined audience that will accept the break in norms. The refusal then invites the second group to pass negative judgment on the first group, or put differently, invites the preconceived incarnation of the audience to become a reinvented audience. Schilb contends, "The refuser begins by assuming that his or her actual audience is the first group. The refuser then tries to show that this group's reasoning is limited. More generally, the refuser works at converting the actual audience into the second group" (39). The reinvented audience, or the second group, is moved to consider a dissociation of terms, typically a dissociation that outright challenges a previously accepted worldview.

Rhetorical refusals require a critical awareness of purpose, audience, doxa, and kairos. This chapter asks, how can teaching rhetorical refusal develop students' awareness of power relations and audience, both "real" audiences and audience as a construct of the author or speaker? Furthermore, how can studying the rhetorical situation and concept of audience in textual artifacts invoke reflection in students to consider audience in their own writing? Schilb writes, "I believe, for example, [students] should know that rhetorical refusals have happened. They would also benefit from seeing these moves as possible for themselves. Of course, the recognition comes more readily if they try out these strategies. But practice needs to be joined by reflection" (177). Students can learn to recognize rhetorical refusals in other artifacts and in doing so learn to utilize rhetorical refusals themselves. Students need to reflect on both their own use and their recognition of refusal in other artifacts as a way to further develop awareness of audience in the rhetorical refusal situation.

Before delving further into the teaching of audience, in the next section I emphasize the elements of drama and risk in rhetorical refusals as aspects that can highlight underlying power relations. I then lay out debates about the concept of audience in rhetorical studies. I conclude with a lesson plan based on chapter four, where Jewish student activists refuse maps of "Greater Israel" dispersed on Birthright trips that fail to demarcate the occupied Palestinian territories. What rhetorical work is the Greater Israel map doing? What rhetorical work are student activists engaging when they refuse such maps? Who is the audience of this refusal and how does it spark reflection?

Drama in the Classroom

Depending on the situation, rhetorical refusals can be quite risky. In the case of Israel and Palestine, there are severe constraints and challenges associated with political dissent for Jews seeking to advance Palestinian rights in a public sphere that is hostile to the humanization of Israel's supposed enemies, let alone for Palestinians speaking up for their own rights. Since refusals with regard to Palestinian liberation entail this element of drama, teaching refusals in this context of constraints and risk can spark reflection *and* a sense of curiosity to motivate learning. Berthoff questions the linguistic assumptions of problem solving and its influence on composition research and argues for an English pedagogy that embraces drama in the classroom: dialectics, repetition and opposition, rhetorical analysis, poetics, and interpretive skill. She writes, "Drama in the classroom could help us begin with where our students are as knowers;

drama could help our students develop conceptions of language as an instrument of knowing. It could help teachers grasp the implications of the fact that knowing in the classroom is a joint enterprise" ("From Problem-solving" 643). Berthoff emphasizes language as an instrument of knowledge with the "capacity to be exercised, not one that must be instilled" ("From Problem-solving" 648). Abraham, and rhetoricians Jonathan Alexander and Susan C. Jarratt have examined rhetorical refusals among voices of dissent for Palestinian rights that demonstrate an awareness of context, audience, and worldview. Abraham's analysis entails a Palestinian American dissenter, and Alexander and Jarratt's case study includes five Muslim American student activists. Taken together, their case studies elucidate an analysis of power relations in a rhetorical refusal situation that highlight the privileging of certain voices over others.

Abraham's analysis illustrates how the refusal to engage with one's political opposition helps to morally clarify the author's or speaker's viewpoint. The force of moral clarity of a rhetorical refusal can risk backlash and material consequences when the dominant audience takes offense to the refusal. This element of drama can capture students' interests as they begin to understand the facets of a refusal situation. In his case study, Abraham examines tweets by Palestinian American scholar and activist Steven Salaita during the 2014 Gaza War, where Salaita utilized critical language so provocative according to the dominant narrative that he was denied a tenured academic appointment that had been approved at all levels, with the exception of the Board of Trustees at the University of Illinois at Urbana-Champaign (UIUC). As a concrete example of a controversial rhetorical refusal, Salaita's case and Abraham's analysis illuminate the ways in which dominant ideology naturalizes itself as the taken for granted reality. In his theory of audience as the "Second Persona," rhetorician Edwin Black argues for an understanding of primary audience that is shaped through the ideology of the message. As I discussed in chapter one, in a given rhetorical situation the First Persona is the author or speaker, and the Second Persona is the intended audience for the author's or speaker's message. In this sense, ideology is rhetorically transmitted through the message, which then works to constitute the worldview and identity of the intended audience, or Second Persona. Interestingly, by refusing to engage with the Second Persona and speaking directly to the Third Persona, Salaita reconstitutes the Second Persona by revealing the language of justification that the dominant ideology otherwise seeks to conceal.

Salaita's tweets show both the power of disrupting the dominant narrative along with the risks entailed in doing so. Abraham argues, "Salaita's tweets counter and expose this discourse of [Israeli] exceptionalism by making Zionism's ideological commitments visible, especially with respect to the precariousness of Palestinian lives" ("Steven Salaita's" 80). Abraham surveys a collection of Salaita's tweets over the course of about three months during the war and shows how Salaita leverages his platform on Twitter to rhetorically refuse Zionist justification for the carnage. By refusing the ideology and refusing to engage with those who espouse it, Salaita in effect exposes how Zionism as the dominant ideology justifies the violence it requires to maintain itself as such. Moreover, Abraham shows how Salaita appeals to a higher moral ground; through the refusal, Salaita's own position is morally clarified. In one example of a tweet, Salaita writes: "Hit the block button, friends, it's pointless to argue with somebody who's okay with bombing schools, hospitals, and shelters" (qtd. in Abraham, "Steven Salaita's" 84). In his critical assessment of power relations in this rhetorical situation, Abraham shows how threatening Salaita's tweets are to the dominant narrative when Palestinian resistance refuses its own denial of humanity according to the discourses of Israeli exceptionalism.

In his tweet "Hit the block button, friends," Salaita invokes two audiences. One audience is the group he refuses to argue with, the dominant group who would justify Israel's bombing of Gaza's schools, hospitals, and shelters. The second audience is "friends," the group who adheres to Salaita's refusal, and whom Salaita invites to pass judgment on the first group. Salaita's status as a tenured professor added cultural and political currency to his tweets' rhetorical refusal of Zionism and refusal to engage in argument, so much so that he was denied a tenured appointment for speaking out so powerfully against Israel's actions. Salaita's case poignantly demonstrates the constraints and challenges of rhetorical refusal, and how refusal can entail significant symbolic and material risk.

In their case study, Alexander and Jarratt point out the limits of refusal to engage in argument as a protest strategy. They also show how differing intervention strategies into dominant narratives entail risk. Alexander and Jarratt conduct interviews with five Muslim American student activists who were a part of what came to be known as the "Irvine 11." In their interviews, Alexander and Jarratt are interested in the student activists' rhetorical education that informed their decisions for their protest. As a concrete example for analysis in the writing classroom, the "Irvine 11" group could demonstrate the many ways that student activists strategize protest in public debate. For instance, Alexander and Jarratt show how, initially, the student activists employed refusal when politically conservative speakers would come to campus who supported Israeli military actions in the West Bank and Gaza Strip. The students would refuse to attend the speaking events as a form of protest, what Alexander and Jarratt argue was "a pointed denial of their significance by a refusal to engage, or an attempt to call attention, through silence, to what is *not* represented" (534, *original emphasis*). The students reflect on how rhetorical refusal can be utilized as a protest strategy and also the limits of refusal depending on the context and occasion of the event.

The student activists decided that the refusal to engage seemed ineffective for the occasion. Instead, they chose to engage as a form of disruption. The activists staged an intervention at a public speaking event by Michael Oren, then-Israel ambassador to the U.S., by attending the event and repeatedly standing up and interrupting the speaker. In their interviews, the student activists reflected on the power imbalance of the public event in terms of the speaker's power to have the university platform to deliver his message. They felt that "the inequity in the speaking situation and the seriousness of the topic demanded a different form of engagement" (Alexander and Jarratt 535). Although supporters of the "Irvine 11" student activists argued that the students were exercising their First Amendment rights, the students' direct intervention entailed serious risk as they faced legal prosecution for disrupting the event. They were first disciplined by the University of California, Irvine and they were later also prosecuted and convicted of misdemeanor charges. This rhetorical situation requires a rethinking of displays of anger and protest as a deliberate strategy, especially when that anger and protest comes from Muslim students and directed against an Israeli official.

Pedagogically posing the two cases side by side can engage students' imaginations and challenge preconceived notions of the rhetorical situation as an equation to be solved. From Salaita's tweets to the Irvine 11, students could begin to see how meaning is contested—i.e., notions of the real—and the way asymmetrical power relations function in a situation that can affect the choices made by a refuser. Problem-posing education understands the human brain as an organ, not a computer. Like other muscles, the brain needs to be stretched with challenging exercises in order to grow and strengthen. Berthoff approaches the problem of meaning in discourse and the teaching of English from a theory of imagination that sees language as an instrument of knowledge; language shapes realities and builds worlds. Transactional problem solving, not open-ended problem posing, presumes human persons to be "encoding-decoding machine[s]," whereas a theory of imagination recognizes the human as *animal symbolicum*, a "creature whose world of behavior is built by language and who makes sense of 'reality' by a process of linguistic invention and discrimination" ("From Problem-solving" 638). Moreover, these cases highlight the elements of risk and consequence when rhetors decide to publicly confront dominant ideologies with alternative or opposing viewpoints. Salaita was denied his tenured appointment at UIUC, and the Irvine 11 were arrested and charged with misdemeanor counts of conspiracy and disruption. Before I present a lesson plan that offers a heuristic and concrete example to students of a rhetorical refusal as a way to develop audience analysis and awareness of power relations, in the next section I examine different pedagogical approaches to the teaching of audience in the writing classroom.

Audience Analysis and Writing Pedagogy

Not only do instructors strive to develop audience awareness for students in the analysis of rhetorical artifacts, but also for students' own writing process and essay assignments. Writing pedagogy theorists such as Andrea A. Lunsford, Lisa Ede, and Irene L. Clark variously argue for such a connection between rhetorical analysis of audience in an artifact and audience awareness in one's own writing process. The connection is not inherent but must be cultivated and made explicit by the writing instructor to help students reflect on the rhetorical significance of audience in a critical manner.

Audience as Invoked

As I discussed chapter four, the concept of audience is integral to Schilb's theory of

rhetorical refusal. Schilb takes a Perelmanian approach to audience that balances between

"actual" audiences and audience as a construct of the author or speaker, or the particular

audience and universal audience. While the Perelmanian philosophy of rhetoric positions the

universal audience as an ideal, Ede and Lunsford develop a somewhat transactional heuristic of

"audience as addressed" and "audience as invoked" (156, 160). Compositionists Linda Adler-

Kassner and Elizabeth Wardle look at audience as a threshold concept in the way that it entails

both the "actual" (addressed) and the imagined (invoked) audience. This can be a challenging

configuration for students to understand. In their Introduction to *Naming What We Know*, Adler-

Kassner and Wardle argue that "threshold concepts are liminal, and learning them happens over

time at varied levels of understanding. They often cannot be taught directly by explication but

must be experienced and enacted over time with others before they are fully understood" (8).[64] In

this way, by examining a series of cases of rhetorical refusal situations and then experimenting

with the invention of refusal themselves, students can work through audience as a threshold

concept and begin to incorporate a higher order of reasoning.

The notion of "audience as invoked" is framed as a construct of the author or speaker.

Although this framing can reinforce a transactional, problem-solving approach, it can also be

utilized as a starting point to meet students where they are. Educators necessarily construct the

dyad for students, only to then deconstruct and dissolve false dichotomies. For instance, literary

---

[64] *Naming What We Know* is a composite work of mini-chapters or entries by various scholars in writing studies who define or outline the threshold concepts of the field. In Kevin Roozen's entry for the threshold concept "Writing is a Social and Rhetorical Activity," he contends, "Writers are always doing the rhetorical work of addressing the needs and interests of a particular audience, even if unconsciously" (in Adler-Kassner and Wardle 17). Roozen argues further, "If teachers can help students consider their potential audiences and purposes, they can better help them understand what makes a text effective or not, what it accomplishes, and what it falls short of accomplishing" (Adler-Kassner and Wardle 18).

philosopher Walter J. Ong presents a transactional approach that distinguishes between actual audiences in front of a speaker versus a collective of individual readers separated in time and space. Ong argues, "For the speaker, the audience is in front of him. For the writer, the audience is simply further away, in time or space or both" (10). According to Ong's concept of audience, the reader takes up the role that the writer has constructed through textual cues. Ong contends, "Readers over the ages have had to learn this game of literacy, how to conform themselves to the projections of the writers they read[.] … They have to know how to play the game of being a member of an audience that 'really' does not exist" (12). In this sense, the writer creates a role for the reader in a shared assumption of what the reader already knows or imagines.

Writers fictionalize their readers, and the reader takes up the fictionalized role for themselves according to "implicit signals" in the text (12). Ong illustrates this role play between writer and reader in an excerpt from Ernest Hemingway's *A Farewell to Arms*. Ong shows how the writer suggests to the reader, through the use of definite articles and demonstrative pronouns ("that year," "the river," "the mountains,"—what year? what river? which mountains?), the assumed role the reader takes. Ong argues, "Hemingway's exclusion of indefinite in favor of definite articles signals the reader that he is from the first on familiar ground. … The reader must pretend he has known much of it before" (13). Through certain cues in the narrative, the writer develops a relationship with the reader according to the fictionalized role the writer determines. Ong shows how this type of relationship takes shape among different authors, such as with Faulkner, who "demands more skilled and daring readers" (14).

According to Ong, unless the rhetorical and literary situation involves an actual speaker with a real-life audience, such as oral storytellers or any type of public speaking, the author's audience is not really an audience, but a composite collectivity of fictionalized readers across time and space. Ong insists that "the writer's audience is always a fiction. The historian, the scholar or scientist, and the simple letter writer all fictionalize their audiences, casting them in a made-up role and calling on them to play the role assigned" (17). The writer "enforce[s]" a role on the reader (18). In this way, the relationship between writer and reader is conceptualized as unidirectional. Ong does not account for the reader's agency in co-creating meaning with the writer, or the analyst as an interpreter of the interpretation; rather, the reader submits to the role the writer constructs in order to follow along with what the author narrates. On the type of relationship between interpreter and text, as mentioned earlier Berthoff questions the approach of "problem solving" in rhetorical and literary studies, which assumes language as a binary code to be encoded by the writer and decoded by the reader ("From Problem-Solving" 638). She argues against this approach and that the relation between author, audience, and analyst is a triadic, contextually specific scenario of meaning making and pedagogical interpretation.

Berthoff takes on what I. A. Richards calls "gangster theories," which reduce the study of language to the arbitrary sign and discourse as binary code, and "tend to focus on words out of context" ("Problem-Dissolving" 10). Dyadic semiotics, Berthoff argues, "make[s] teaching impossible by undercutting attempts to keep the making of meaning central" ("Problem-Dissolving" 10). Berthoff insists upon the notion of triadicity which includes the interpretant, "the idea which mediates the representation and what it represents." In other words, Berthoff understands "interpretation as a constituent of the sign," or the signifier and signified "as a relationship mediated by interpretation" ("Problem-Dissolving" 9). Triadicity insists upon words in context, or interpretation of interpretation, in order to understand meaning and its relationship to knowledge. Triadicity implicates the reader as the interpretant (i.e., the effect of a sign on someone who reads or comprehends it) in meaning-making, rather than strictly assuming a fictionalized and unidirectional role constructed for the reader by the writer. Furthermore, through a triadic problem-posing pedagogy, students can begin to see how the writer may have certain motives and goals for their message, and certain implicit directives for the role of the reader cued in the text, yet the audience can receive or reconstruct that message differently than originally intended by the writer.[65]

As a starting point for students' understanding, a transactional approach to audience analysis can develop an awareness of ideology in the given rhetorical situation. For example, Black contends that stylistic tokens, such as metaphors, vivid language, and other symbolisms, can work to convey an ideology through the claims that are made (112). The Second Persona then becomes constituted as a particular audience which "determin[es] how he views the world" (112). How is rhetoric functioning to convey a certain ideology and influence the intended audience as such? Moreover, what kind of judgments can then be made regarding the rhetorical work of pervasive, dominant ideologies? Black illustrates the function of second persona through a rhetorical analysis of Cold War "Radical Right" ideology that claims Communism is a cancer. Through the symbolism of Communism as cancer, Black argues that "the topos and the metaphor are examples of an idiomatic token of ideology" (115). Significantly, this analysis reveals how the metaphor separates the intended audience from a foreign Other who is demonized through the stylistic token in the message. Audience analysis of the Second Persona demonstrates the ways in which ideological rhetoric can construct an "us versus them" binary opposition. Black's audience analysis might assume a linear communicative model where the author or speaker

---

[65] In his entry in *Naming What We Know*, Charles Bazerman explains the threshold concept "Writing Expresses and Shares Meaning to be Reconstructed by the Reader," which takes a multidirectional view of the relationship between writer and reader. Rather than necessarily falling into the fictionalized role that the writer signals for the reader to decode, the reader reconstructs meaning from text "based on what they already know" (in Adler-Kassner and Wardle 22). In other words, readers bring their prior knowledges, worldviews, and experiences to the interpretation of a text.

transmits a message to the audience, as though the audience is a passive receptacle into which the fictionalized role may be deposited. However, utilized pedagogically as one aspect of analysis, the Second Persona can help students begin to see the way that unspoken but reinforced norms circulate in public discourse as a way to maintain a certain order.

Audience as Discourse Community

Departing from current-traditional and expressivist rhetorics of audience that emphasize the role of the writer in creating meaning in the text, rhetorician James Porter takes up a social constructionist and poststructuralist view of audience in the rhetorical situation that sees audience in terms of a discourse community. In his conception of the discourse community, the role between author or speaker and audience is blurred; Porter argues that "the audience is a 'discourse community' constraining, defining, and in effect creating the writer. 'The writer' is a role, a subject position, constituted by community constraints" (83). In this model, in order for the writer to become a writer in a discourse community, they must familiarize themselves with the values, principles, and genre conventions of the community. In this way, the writer and the audience are dialectically constituted through the given discourse community, and the writer is part and parcel of the audience just as much as when they become an author or speaker of the discourse.

To teach this concept of audience, Porter advocates for "forum analysis" to help students understand the rhetorical aspects of discourse communities (137). Forums, such as journals, newsletters, conferences, and the like, can provide a concrete example of the interrelation of author or speaker and audience for students where the forum represents a larger discourse community. In *Genre Analysis*, linguist John Swales offers a heuristic of distinct roles and aspects of the discourse community that emphasize a community's common set of goals, conventions or lexis, and "participatory mechanisms" for writers and audience members to engage with a given community (25). Swales argues that "individuals enter [discourse communities] as apprentices" and develop their expertise as writers over time (27). Porter remains interested in the ways that discourse communities constitute their authors or speakers and audiences as such, while Swales offers practical characterizations of discourse communities influenced by a sociolinguistic framework.

Disrupting from Within

Rhetorician Alan Gross revisits Perelman's theory of rhetorical audience and argues that, through adherence to the order of the rhetor's discourse, the universal audience is transformed (influenced) from beginning to end of the argument. In other words, the author or speaker begins with a claim or a set of truths and values and carries the audience through the argument to prove the claim and thus successfully produce the desired effect in the audience. The universal audience may believe one thing at the beginning of an argument and be led to believe another, depending on the goal of the message (to educate? to persuade and inform? to inspire?). Regarding the larger debate about actual audiences and constructed, invoked, fictionalized, imagined audiences, Gross writes, "Of course there are real audiences; of course their study poses a genuine problem; but it is a challenge, he [Perelman] feels, beyond the scope of rhetoric: the study of real audiences is the business of experimental psychology. … This necessity means that the rhetorician is dependent on, not independent of experimental psychology" (204). On this point, Porter asks, "Is there ever an exact correspondence between imagined audience and real reader?" (4). Porter points to the troublesome aspect of audience as a threshold concept in rhetoric and writing studies, that rhetorical audiences are both real and imagined.

While Schilb utilizes a Perelmanian approach to audience in his theory of rhetorical refusal, the concept of discourse community can also be applied. In this frame, rhetorical refusals occur when author or speaker breaks with genre conventions or the norms of discourse in a given community, or, ideologically speaking, refusals occur when author or speaker rejects dominant narratives that may be already accepted by the primary audience in a discourse community. Schilb argues, "They [rhetors] reject a move their audience expects for one supposedly more virtuous" (39). In an appeal to higher moral ground, the goal of the refusal is to reframe conceptions of the real that are naturalized by the dominant worldview, to show the audience an alternative way of seeing, as it were.

In addition to the Salaita and Irvine 11 cases, the case of Israeli conscientious objectors can provide students a rhetorical refusal situation with an accessible context of clearly defined roles. In this context of Israeli militarism and what anthropologist Erica Weiss calls its sacrificial economy, IDF soldiers who speak out or conscientiously object risk paying a heavy price. For one, in Israel, the "refusal by qualified individuals to perform military service is illegal" (Weiss 576). Refusal to join the military can and often means serving time in military prison. It also entails ridicule and harassment from politicians and the media in addition to possible ostracization from personal and public communities.[66] Unsurprisingly, IDF soldiers who speak out after their service or who conscientiously refuse to serve have been condemned as traitors. If the refusers do not speak out and remain silent as the sacrificial economy demands, the price they pay might be even higher—their sanity and sense of self. In his video testimonial, "Why I

---

[66] In her ethnography *Conscientious Objectors in Israel*, Erica Weiss writes about a soldier named Amos, who "insisted that the worst moment in his life was when he sat in his family's living room and told his father that, after many years serving in the military, he planned to sign a letter of refusal to serve. ... After that encounter, it was more than a year before he spoke with his father again. ... [T]he rift was very difficult for Amos, who had enjoyed his tight-knit family and their emotional and material support" (3–4).

break the silence," IDF veteran Zohar Shapira discusses how he felt he was a different person as a solider in the occupied territories compared to the person he was when he came home to his wife and children. He says: "You're a different person and you can't mix the two. You can't be a psychopath and a lover…in the same body. … I repressed it into darkness under pressure. You refused to see reality and then it surfaces." Shapira is referring to the "reality" that the Israeli national narrative and sacrificial economy refuses to see, the inhumane routine maintenance of the occupation. Rhetorical refusals such as Shapira's, where he refuses to remain silent about injustice, "epitomize[s] dissociation," what Schilb says can have the power to "explode an ideal" (34). In this way, students can begin to see the notion of refusal operating at several levels: the refusal to serve, the refusal to remain silent, and the dominant ideology's refusal to "see reality."

Moreover, for first- and second-year college students who have recently graduated high school, students can learn about the *Shministim* movement (*Shministim* is Hebrew for "twelfth graders") and potentially identify with young refusers who could be around the same age. As recent as 2021, the *Shministim* released a public letter declaring their conscientious objection to military service in the occupied territories. As a study of rhetorical refusal, students could analyze the public letter, editorials or comments in Israeli society responding to the letter to discern audience reception, in addition to screening the 2021 documentary film *Objector: From an Israeli Rite of Passage to a Battle for Human Rights* to help establish critical context of Israeli militarism and compulsory enlistment. The Jewish Film Institute describes the documentary: "*Objector* follows Atalya through her conscientious objection, imprisonment, and beyond, as she attempts to reconcile her Jewish identity, her love for her homeland, and her dedication to Palestinian rights. Her courage moves those around her to reconsider their own political positions and power to effect change" ("Objector"). The *Shministim* public letter entailed a collective writing process for over a year, where refusers would meet once or twice a week to think through their statement. Their main goal is to encourage other young Israelis to think about how they are taking a part of the occupation by enlisting, and to make the issue debatable.

Audience as Source of Invention

As previously mentioned, Ede and Lunsford conceptualize audience in a transactional fashion, as "addressed" and "invoked" (156, 160). Ede and Lunsford argue against an overemphasis on either or in writing pedagogy; they believe actual audiences and imagined audiences must be taught in a balanced way and not pitted against one another. In pedagogical models of audience that place too much emphasis on audience as addressed, "the audience has the sole power of evaluating writing" (158). Ede and Lunsford see the potential for audience as a source of invention for writers in the composing process. However, in its "extreme form," overemphasizing audience as addressed "becomes pandering to the crowd" and "tends to undervalue the responsibility a writer has to a subject" (159). On the other end of the spectrum, overemphasis on audience as invoked fails to capture the complexity of audience discernment in the writing process. Ede and Lunsford contend that writers "*both* analyze and invent an audience" (163, *original emphasis*). Whereas overemphasis on audience as addressed places an imbalanced amount of power on the audience to control the meaning communicated in a text, on the opposing side "it distorts the process of writing and reading by overemphasizing the power of the writer and undervaluing that of the reader" (165). Audience as addressed and invoked must be viewed not as a dichotomy but as a synthesis between the two.

In their proposed model, Ede and Lunsford illustrate their synthesized approach through the image of a wheel with the writer at the center and lines extending as spokes around the circle to possible audiences as addressed and invoked. Invoked audience roles include self, friend, colleague, critic, mass audience, future audience, past audience, and anomalous audience; addressed audience roles include future audience, mass audience, critic, colleague, friend, self (166). Ede and Lunsford's model shows how overlapping audience roles are both actual and imagined. They argue, "The addressed audience, the actual or intended readers of a discourse, exists outside of the text. … But it is only through the text, through language, that writers embody or give life to their conception of the reader." Differentiating themselves from Ong's fictionalized reader, they add, "In so doing, they [writers] do not so much create a role for the reader—a phrase which implies that the writer somehow creates a mold to which the reader adapts—as invoke it" (167). Ede and Lunsford advocate for a view of audience that recognizes the ways both writers and readers invent and interpret the meaning in a text in its rhetorical situation.

In *Concepts in Composition*, Clark similarly argues that writing pedagogies of audience need to help students make connections between real and invented audiences, in addition to other aspects of the text such as purpose, form, style, and genre (141). While teaching students about audience through concrete examples may be one thing, it is another for students to reflect on the role of audience in their own process. Moreover, the writing classroom poses a distinct evaluative situation for students where a student's final product is assessed by the instructor. In this way, Clark points out that students often view their audience or reader as the teacher, and their goal is to meet the required expectations of a given essay assignment to appease the instructor. Although it is true that one immediate reader of a student essay is the instructor (and the peer reviewer), and the essay will necessarily be evaluated for a grade, the college composition classroom nonetheless strives to push students beyond this student-to-teacher writer-reader dyad toward broader conceptions of writing, rhetoric, audience, purpose, and context.

Clark presents different models of audience such as compositionist James Moffett's "universe of discourse," which postulates a progression of audience awareness for students where they begin with writing for themselves, to communicating a story or recreating the experience of an event to a close friend, to narrating a story or writing to inform or persuade for a public audience. Clark argues, "The teacher's role within this universe is to construct writing assignments that enable students to move in this progression and to gain consciousness of how different audiences require different conceptual and textual strategies" (146). While Clark does contend that "examining texts for audience-based cues can help students understand the concept more fully" (156), she also maintains that "this hoped-for carryover rarely happens when students write their own essays" (155). In order for this "hoped-for carryover" to happen, composition instructors must help students to not only analyze concrete scenarios of audience in textual artifacts but also reflect on actual demographics for intended audiences in their writing. Clark recommends an audience demographic analysis activity for students to consider their own audience but admits that one downfall of this activity is that it can slide into stereotypes of audience characteristics. Nonetheless, she recommends students conduct research about the demographics of a given audience and assess their values and interests. Clark offers this "Audience Analysis Sheet" (156) for students to consider:

1. Who is my audience? What knowledge about the subject does my audience already have?

2. What does my audience think, believe, or understand about this topic before he or she reads my essay?

3. What do I want my audience to think, believe, or understand about this topic after he or she reads my essay?

4. How do I want my audience to think of me?

I would add a fifth question to this analysis sheet: How do I want my audience to think of themselves? This type of question might help students reflect on the ways in which they "invoke" an audience at the same time that they are addressing an audience. What kind of textual cues and rhetorical appeals could a student employ to shape an audience's view of itself as a way to effectively communicate the message?

While Clark's survey of the concept of audience in the composition classroom offers several activities to utilize audience as a source of invention for students, compositionist Peter Elbow famously argues that in the early stages of drafting perhaps students should forget audience altogether. He contends that if instructors overemphasize the role of audience in the writing process during the brainstorming and early drafting phase, students may feel stifled by thinking too much about how to attend to their audience. Elbow argues that some audiences are "*inviting* or *enabling*" while others are "powerfully *inhibiting*" (51, *original emphases*). He contends that students should learn to consider their audience later on in the writing process during the revision stages after "copious exploratory draft writing—perhaps finding the right voice or stance as well" (52). Elbow advocates for an expressivist approach to developing voice, for students to spend time learning about themselves and what they think before learning how to effectively communicate their stance to an intended audience.

Clark similarly contends that students can learn more about audience awareness in their own writing during the later stages. She writes, "Peer feedback is one of the most useful strategies I know for helping students gain awareness of audience" (157). As I will show in the framing of my lesson plan in the next section, teaching audience analysis through rhetorical refusal combines these pedagogical strategies in a scaffolded way. Students study refusals in concrete examples (as Ede and Lunsford and Clark suggest), and then attempt to write rhetorical refusals themselves (suggested by Schilb). Before considering their own audience in the refusal situation, I heed Elbow's advice for students to engage in meaningful exploratory writing for them to gain a sense of their own voice and stance.

In *Upsetting Composition Commonplaces*, rhetorician Ian Barnard interrogates the ways in which writing pedagogy can perpetuate a reductive and problematic conception of audience in typical essay assignment genres such as academic essays, argumentative essays, and persuasive essays. Barnard argues that the skeptical "general audience" that a writer tries to persuade is a commonplace in college writing classrooms that in effect constrains and takes away from exploratory, non-thesis-driven, pleasurable aspects of writing. By focusing on the anticipation of counter claims and goals of persuading the skeptical audience, this liberal pluralist commonplace reduces an otherwise complex and multifaceted writing process to a pro/con binary with an intended outcome of achieving consensus and conformity. Barnard critically contends that "this audience imperative is implicated in creating and enforcing bourgeois and other politically inflected conceptualizations and parameters of discourse and civility, and thus can be seen as advancing the idea of composition as a space for teaching students how to accommodate themselves to corporate capitalism" (112). As an arena for political discourse and ideological representations, Barnard reminds us that mainstream media platforms and news outlets (often seen by students as the "general audience") are funded and owned by corporate conglomerates that dictate in insidious ways how and what ideas and information gets taken up and circulated.

The "conjuring of a putatively hostile but potentially persuadable reader" as a type of universal, general audience in writing classrooms can inadvertently perpetuate ideologically laden conceptions of universality to which students must conform in their attempts to reach this seemingly "general" audience through their argumentative essays (Barnard 117). As an engaging counterdiscourse writing assignment, Barnard teaches students about zines and how to make them. Zines create a unique opportunity for students to speak not to a skeptical audience but to a radically agreeable audience that can allow for transgressive and passionate expressions of viewpoints. Moreover, Barnard encourages a tangible form of audience awareness through the zine assignment by having students create their own zines and then distribute them to their intended audience. As best as they can, students are asked to gauge their audience's reaction to the zine. Barnard argues, "Work with zines not only enables students to escape the ideological dictates of liberal pluralism [which demands consensus and proper decorum], but also serves an immediate pedagogical function by giving them a much sharper and more immediate sense of their readers" (121). Zines can also help elucidate the concept of audience as discourse community for students, which I believe is an important approach for teaching rhetorical refusal and audience discernment.

For students to bridge the gap between analyzing concrete situations of audience and refusal in a textual artifact toward utilizing the strategy and discernment for themselves in their own writing, the concept of audience as discourse community can play a pivotal role for students to comprehend the troublesome aspect of audience as *both* addressed and invoked. In addition, rhetorical refusal can complicate the commonplace of pro/con binary argumentation that Barnard is so critical of by focusing on how dominant and marginalized narratives circulate within communities through asymmetrical relations of power. By analyzing refusal, students can come to see how dominant narratives may circulate in a given community as the norm, or as a naturalized form of ideology that rhetorically consolidates power for a hegemonic worldview. Refusal works to disrupt this hegemony and intervene with an alternative way of seeing. Furthermore, teaching rhetorical refusal can expose how language is socially constructed and how "discourse community" functions an unstable and fluid identity category, not reducible to a dominant narrative that sets a privileged norm. Refusal can offer a critical lens for ideological analyses of how rhetoric is functioning, and the ways in which language circulates among communities with social power to persuade, convince, and reify.

Contextualizing the Curriculum

While I offer a lesson plan of the map of Greater Israel (see fig. 9) based on my research from chapter four, students should be exposed to a range of examples of rhetorical refusals to see how they operate in different contexts. The controversy around then-NFL quarterback Colin Kaepernick taking a knee during the National Anthem could be a case study of rhetorical refusal. Commonly taught in first-year writing courses, Dr. King's "Letter from Birmingham Jail" can be reframed through the lens of refusal to help students appreciate the depth of the textual artifact's rhetorical situation. As a canonical refutation to the "Call for Unity" statement by eight white Alabama clergymen, Dr. King refuses what he calls the myth of time, or, being told to wait. Examining "Letter from Birmingham Jail" as a rhetorical refusal can offer a fresh take on the artifact and help students understand the concept of audience as addressed and invoked. In his book, Schilb offers several case studies of rhetorical refusals, which he suggests could be studied by students (177). His case studies range from dance critic Arlene Croce's refusal to see *Still/Here*, to historian Deborah Lipstadt's refusal to debate a Holocaust denier, to an 1876 speech by Frederick Douglass about Abraham Lincoln. In the lesson plan that follows, I offer the concrete example of the Greater Israel map for students to consider as a case study, and then I lay out a heuristic for instructors to use with students to try composing a rhetorical refusal themselves. To finish, I suggest a metacognitive activity for students to reflect on these analytical and composing processes to help further develop audience discernment and to help bridge the gap between textual analysis and one's own writing process.

While I offer the two-part lesson plan here, I position the concrete example of the refusal of Greater Israel maps in a larger unit on rhetorical analysis of controversy with multiple examples of rhetorical refusal as a way for students to research and explore political controversy. In the scope of the semester-long curriculum, I situate the controversy analysis unit after the introductory unit on genre analysis of a discourse community, topics which students research and select themselves. Ideally, students select a discourse community with which they identify or that they are curious about potentially joining. Students select their topic or discourse community with the first unit and major essay assignment, and then stick with this topic through the semester. The controversy analysis unit builds upon the research of their discourse community by further examining a political controversy specific to that community. I offer the framework of rhetorical refusal to students as one way to approach their controversy analysis. If anything, I am interested in the ways that rhetorical refusals can help students develop audience discernment in their own analyses and writing processes, whether they end up identifying a case of refusal in their discourse community or not. I present the case studies of refusal to the class to help students develop an analytical toolkit to bring to their own research.

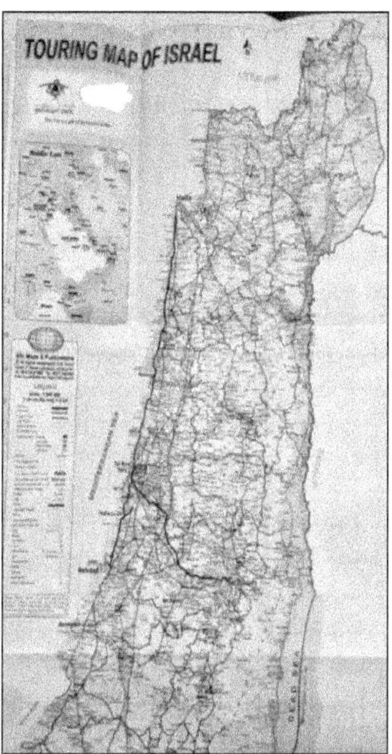

Fig. 9. Birthright map of Israel that fails to mark the occupied West Bank, making it look like the West Bank is naturally a part of Israel proper (photo: Bethany Zaiman from her piece in *The Nation*).

Lesson plan 1 of 2, "Exploratory Writing and Textual Analysis"

Time length: Fifty minutes

Content:

- "I'm One of the Young People Who Walked Off Birthright Israel This Summer" by Bethany Zaiman in *The Nation*: https://www.thenation.com/article/archive/im-one-of-the-young-people-who-walked-off-birthright-israel-this-summer/

- Birthright map of Greater Israel

- The IfNotNow website and the group's four demands for Birthright

Free-write (five min.)

- Start class with an exploratory free-write about the larger theme of "borders."

- Prompt: Are borders rhetorical? How can borders be persuasive? In your own words, what is the purpose of borders? Who gets to decide how and where to draw borders on a map? Who gets to cross which borders, and who doesn't? Can you think of an example of disputed borders or the re-drawing of borders in recent history other than Israel and Palestine?

Pair and share (ten min.)

- Have students turn to a classmate to share their thoughts from the free-write.

Class reflection (ten min.)

- Class discussion to share what they discussed in pairs. I recommend writing highlights or themes from the discussion on the board for students to see.

Mini lecture to provide context (ten min.)

- Brief background about disputed borders in Israel and Palestine (such as key dates 1948 and 1967, and point to the West Bank and Gaza Strip).

- Review the article in *The Nation* (students read before class, assigned for homework).

Class discussion of rhetorical refusal situation (fifteen min.)

- Questions for analysis:

    o Who are the authors or speakers of the refusal?

    o What is the message of the refusal?

    o What are their goals with the refusal? What are the activists "refusing" and why?

    o Who is their immediate audience, and what type of audience are they inviting them to become through the refusal (the "reinvented audience" or, according to Schilb, the "second group" which passes judgement on the first group)?

- o What kind of appeal is being made to higher moral ground? What are these morals or values?

- o Is this rhetorical refusal risky? How so?

- o Can you assess the power relations in this rhetorical situation between refuser and audience?

Lesson plan 2 of 2, "Rhetorical Refusal Workshop and Reflection"

Time length: Fifty minutes

Content:

- Students' research from essay one about their topic and discourse community

- BYOD (Bring Your Own Device, aka laptop) for preliminary research

Research activity (ten min.)

- Have students spend some time researching a possible controversy in their discourse community. This lesson plan builds upon previous lessons that conceptualized rhetorical analysis of a controversy. Students have asked themselves, what makes a controversy, a controversy? Now they can start to explore controversies in their chosen research topic and discourse communities.

Class discussion (ten min.)

- What are some controversies you have identified?

- What might a rhetorical refusal look like in your controversy?

Writing activity (fifteen min.)

- Students will experiment in the role of author/speaker in their discourse community amidst the researched controversy. Ask students to write and reflect on the following questions to help them craft their own refusal:

- o What are some of the genre conventions of your discourse community? What are some expectations your audience might have about this controversy? In other words, what are some of the values and beliefs that your discourse community circulates?

- o What might it look like to "refuse" audience expectations and appeal to a higher set of values (e.g., justice, freedom, diversity and inclusion, equality, compassion, kindness, empathy)?

- Have students post their rhetorical refusals to the classroom's online forum.

Pair and share (ten min.)

- Have students turn to a classmate to share their rhetorical refusals. Treat this like a mini-peer review for students to offer one another initial impressions and feedback.

Metacognitive reflection (homework)

- Have students pause and respond to the following questions:
  - o What did you learn about rhetoric through this refusal?
  - o What did you learn about controversy through this process of analysis?
  - o Was it a challenge to experiment as the author/speaker who stages a rhetorical refusal in your discourse community? How so?
  - o What aspects of audience did you consider? Did this help you come up with a refusal? How so?
  - o What was challenging or difficult about this writing activity? Or, what did you enjoy about it?
  - o Do you feel like your initial drafts today could turn into a successful rhetorical refusal with more development? Why or why not?

- Have students post their reflection memos to the classroom's online forum.

See, Do, Reflect

As I mentioned in the above framing of this two-part lesson plan, these lessons are situated in the context of a semester-long curriculum, building upon previous lectures and writing and research workshops that have delved into the "rhetorical situation" (e.g., author/speaker, message and purpose, primary and secondary audience, context, exigence, medium, rhetorical devices and appeals) as a theoretical framework for students utilize for analysis and in their own writing processes. To compliment the rhetorical situation, it is expected prior to these proposed lesson plans that students are also familiar with genre analysis and the notion of discourse community. To build further on this pedagogical development, I would introduce the concept of rhetorical refusal prior to these lessons, and I would offer multiple examples of other refusals for students to see so they can begin to analyze and write refusals themselves.

In this chapter, I have reviewed literature about the rhetorical concept of audience, along with debates about how to teach audience analysis in the writing classroom. I offered a two-part lesson plan for rhetorical which begins with exploratory writing about a larger theme ("borders") in the refusal that we will study (the refusal of the Greater Israel map), then moves to context and analysis of rhetorical refusal in the textual artifacts, followed by a research and writing workshop for students to test out refusals for themselves, concluding with a metacognitive reflection activity that draws conscious awareness to analytical developments and invention strategies.

For me, I always try to keep the class schedule flexible with lesson planning. The two-part lesson presented here could, in my eyes, easily turn into a three- or four-part lesson plan in fifty-minute class periods. The analysis of artifacts could be extended, and the research and writing workshop could also be extended for students to have more time to think through their ideas. The pair and share (mini peer review) of students' own refusals, for instance, could also open up to a larger class discussion for students to share their ideas and research findings with the whole group. I like to do this because then I can offer my own feedback to individual students in front of the class, which models for students how to support their peers in the research and writing process in addition to sparking further reflection for their own work. And finally, while I suggested above that the reflection memo could be done for homework, I also like to take time for this reflection in class if possible. It is important for me to guide students through reflection memos as a practice in mindfulness, where I invite students into the present moment and offer a subtle breathing exercise. This helps to draw students into a growth mindset as they reflect on connections between textual artifacts and their own writing process.

Audience awareness can be developed with invention activities such as a forum analysis (suggested by Porter) or by working through an audience analysis sheet (presented by Clark). Or, if one forgoes audience consideration in the invention phase (suggested by Elbow), students can develop audience awareness during the revision stage especially with peer review. Finally, pausing for metacognitive reflection throughout the writing process and particularly after the final product can be a way to connect audience awareness in analysis and in composition.

Epilogue

In June 2018, when I heard about the first, and then second and third, Birthright walk-offs, I was shocked. As a Jewish woman coming of age with Birthright, I saw these ten-day trips as a rite of passage. When I signed up for my Birthright trip to Israel through the Hillel on campus in 2005, I did not know a thing about the military occupation before or after the trip. I had a Reform Jewish upbringing at Temple Chai in Phoenix, Arizona, from religious school and weekend retreats at Camp Pearlstein, to slipping coins in the Jewish National Fund's blue tzedakah boxes, to my bat mitzvah and then Hebrew High on regular school nights. The State of Israel and Zionism were normalized aspects of my religious culture.

Being an American Jewish teenager, for me, meant listening to The Beatles while making hemp beaded necklaces with my best friend Rachael and braiding each other's hair in the morning before school. In 2005, I did not know about the Second Intifada, the Palestinian popular uprising, that erupted in 2000 and was coming to an end in 2005. While Palestinian and Israeli society lingered in turmoil around me, I travelled unaware in an alternate universe from Tzfat to Tel Aviv to Jerusalem to the Dead Sea on the Birthright tour bus. I learned nothing about Palestinian history and society on the trip. Growing up in synagogue, I never thought twice about the Israeli flag with a Star of David perched next to the American flag not far from the rabbi's pulpit. I never thought twice about the maps of Israel that do not mark the borders of the occupied Palestinian territories of the West Bank and Gaza Strip.

I had just turned nineteen years old. My mother was nervous for me to go on Birthright in fear of the suicide bombings she heard about on cable news. I had a vague notion of "a conflict" in Israel. The suicide bombings felt like a distant but looming threat, something I could not fathom but somehow understood that Israel was the one under attack and acting justly in self-defense, and I was a proud Israel defender. The Birthright trip organizers insisted on our safety and all I had to pay for was getting myself to and from JFK airport in New York City. I was fascinated by the prospect that if I wanted to, there was a Jewish country in the Middle East where I could live and have dual citizenship. This is part of what the term "birthright" advocates for, after all.

Throughout my ten-day trip, I was astounded by how many young Israeli soldiers I saw everywhere with assault rifles casually slung over their shoulders. I was told, "that's just how it is over here," and that every eighteen-year-old Israeli Jew is conscripted for a minimum of two to three years before they can attend college. I would look at them and think, what if that was me? As I got to know our peers in the Israeli military who accompanied the trip (known as the Mifgash, or "encounter"), I even considered the prospect of joining the IDF myself. Or I imagined moving to Israel to live on a kibbutz. My new Israeli Jewish friends promised they would help me out, and that I could stay with them for a while to get settled. I cried at the end of the trip when we had to say goodbye.

When I came back from my Birthright trip in January 2006, I remember wearing my Hebrew University sweatshirt and new Star of David necklace every day. But, from an early age, I have always been interested in politics, government, and social justice. It was simply a matter of time for me to learn the reality for Palestinians. Three years later, after declaring a women's studies minor amidst my evolving political consciousness, Israel's Operation Cast Lead in Gaza was the turning point. Reading headlines and seeing photos of dying Palestinian women and children was unspeakably horrifying. This is not a cliché. My blood ran cold; I was devastated. I felt deeply betrayed and ashamed. I remember researching the local International Jewish Ani-

Zionist Network (IJAN) chapter, but despite my rage at the injustice, I was still too nervous to attend a meeting in fear of how my family or Jewish community would react. While I was scared to attend an IJAN meeting, I bitterly refused to step foot in Hillel or attend synagogue where "pro-Israel" rhetoric flowed seamlessly without a single mention of Palestinian existence.

About two years later, after my mother found out that I attended a protest in support of the Gaza Freedom Flotilla in 2011, she accused me of "turning against everything she raised me to be" and would not speak to me for weeks. For many years through my mid-twenties, I felt that I had to choose between Zionism and anti-Zionism under the false notion that you are either pro-Israel or anti-Jewish. I also felt alienated from synagogue where Israeli flags and Greater Israel maps hung on the walls.

I pursued this dissertation because I wanted to know why. As I have repeatedly mentioned, today there are approximately thirteen million people who live between the Jordan River and the Mediterranean Sea, or the West Bank, Israel proper, and the Gaza Strip, all of which is controlled by Israel. Of the thirteen million, half are Palestinians and half are Israeli Jews. With 6 ½ million Palestinians living under Israeli control—not to mention the millions of Palestinians in refugee camps in neighboring countries or in diaspora around the world—why didn't I learn anything about Palestinian culture on my Birthright tour? Why do the maps of Israel handed out on Birthright and hanging in synagogues erase the borders of occupation? Why is Palestinian existence erased in Israel education and advocacy? Through rhetorical strategies of Palestinian erasure such as decontextualization, false accusations of antisemitism, and a Holocaust-centered worldview, Israeli national security rhetoric enables a view from afar in the American Jewish community of Israel as a morally pure and just nation that can do no wrong.

In this dissertation, I set out with a desire to explore Jewish dissenting rhetoric in support of Palestinian rights primarily within an American Jewish intracommunal rhetorical situation. Drawn from my lived experience along with countless personal stories I have heard and read from other Jews, I wanted to think further about an observable phenomenon whereby "pro-Israel" Jews undergo a transformation of self-understanding with regard to Israel when heeding the call for Palestinian freedom. As I explore in chapter three in the rhetoric of first-person narratives by Beinart and Roy, this transformation of self in relation to the constitutive Other can develop into an ethical relation to alterity that reinvents identity apart from exclusionary ethnonationalist conceptions. This transformation can be a gradual process of awareness and reflection, and it can entail a jolting shock of consciousness that shatters one's previously held belief system. I wanted to explore this rhetoric of identity reinvention in order to better understand alternative possibilities of ethical relationality, as well as to call attention to this growing phenomenon in the American Jewish community.

In chapter one, I begin delineating a rhetorical genealogy of Zionism's erasure of Palestinian life and history. In chapter two, I continue to trace the rhetorical genealogy through the trope of the antisemitic Arab terrorist Other, an effect of what I refer to as Zionist rhetoric of existential threat, and I conclude with a case study of Hertzberg's "An Open Letter to Elie Wiesel." Situated in genealogical context, the case studies of dissent show the imperative for reinventing identity as a way toward justice.

As I just mentioned, chapter three examines first-person identity reconstitution by critics Beinart and Roy. First-person identity constitution analyzes how authors and speakers constitute their identities in discourse through narrative about their personal realities, or what Dana Anderson calls "expressible self-interpretation" (11). I show how a critical rhetoric of first-person narrative can be a transformative cultural resource that reinvents identity as an ethical practice in relation to otherness. I look to the work of Butler for a philosophy of ethical relations.

Chapter four examines the rhetorical refusal of ethnonationalist birthright through the lens of the universal audience. For rhetorical theories of the universal audience, I draw upon the work of Perelman and Olbrechts-Tyteca, Fernheimer, Schilb, and Velasco. In chapter five, I turn toward in the practical application of audience-based pedagogy in the writing classroom as a way to cultivate rhetorical awareness in students.

According to the corpus that I examine across chapters one through five, not only are dissenters speaking out in support of Palestinian rights, but they are also asserting for themselves what it means to be Jewish. Such assertions of reinvented self-understanding challenge the dominant narrative of Jewish identity as unequivocally Zionist: "Israel, right or wrong" (Waxman, *Trouble* 55). Through textual analysis, I show how this rhetoric of dissent redraws the contours of Jewish identity as a mode of ethical relations that heeds the call for Palestinian freedom.

At the heart of this reinvention of identity, Jewish dissenters reframe Holocaust memory and the threat of antisemitism as interconnected with other forms of ethnic and racial prejudice, not uniquely separate from. Through this reframing, the call for justice from the Palestinian "Other" becomes audible. Beinart argues: "Our task in this moment is to imagine a new Jewish identity, one that no longer equates Palestinian equality with Jewish genocide. One that sees Palestinian liberation as integral to our own" ("Yavne"). My research shows that dissenting rhetoric can be a resource for cultural transformation and that the reinvention of identity must also be accounted for when imagining a future of decolonization and cohabitation.

There are pitfalls to this work, including the marginalization and absence of Palestinian voices and self-representation—the very thing I want to counter—when Jewish voices are centralized as protagonists. For instance, Palestinians become reinscribed as a shadow in Beinart's and Roy's narratives like a foil for their own transformation as protagonists. In chapter three, I write: "While Beinart tells the story of Fadel, a disenfranchised, stateless Palestinian father, who lives in the West Bank, he interrupts his personal narrative as a self-identified Jewish Zionist, U.S. citizen, and father." In this way, the politics of recognition can function as a mode of containment that inadvertently reproduces a colonialist power relation of enlightened savior rescuing the helpless victim. Today's American Jewish dissenters speak from a privileged position that "translate" what Palestinians have already been saying for decades. That very translation, which can be seen as an important humanizing gesture, nonetheless relies upon the Other as such to define the Self.

As I move forward with this research, I want to reframe an analysis of identity rhetorics in a dialogic manner that reflects on cultural and political collective action and the co-articulation of belonging—how rhetoricians constitute shared identities, build collective engagement, and mobilize those collectives. What is to be done? How can coalitions be created to take collective action to address these issues? From here, I want to begin focusing on a more action-oriented rhetoric of how people build coalitions and mobilize. How do we build factions, not necessarily a consensus or agreement? The modernist rhetorical tradition that I draw upon in my dissertation presumes that universal principles are vested in the norms of liberal debate, whereby Palestinian self-expression becomes legible and audible within a set of parameters that have already been determined.

Since I have pursued a doctorate degree and a dissertation about Israel, Zionism, and Jewish American rhetoric of dissent, my mother has felt less threatened by my criticism and listens far more. I have also come a long way in my relationship with the mainstream Jewish community and affiliation with my local synagogue. My interest in rhetoric of identity comes from my belief that the types of stories we tell about ourselves and who we are have the power to shape the world around us.

Let's ask ourselves, what is to be done? How do we write old stories anew? While Holocaust-centered Zionist rhetoric continues to claim that Jews in the Diaspora need the State of Israel for Jewish security, Israel also frames its geopolitical position as constantly under antisemitic existential threat and attack. Regardless, for many Jews, the State of Israel represents a necessary place of safety and refuge. Of course, I grew up with a deep-seated belief that Israel is a miraculous founding of a nation-state for Jews and is an essential place for Jewish safety. Does Jewish safety require the systematic persecution of the Palestinian people? Must Jewish safety come at the cost of total dehumanization and degradation of Palestinians?

As much as ethnonationalist discourse would like to dictate and cement a certain type of identity narrative as fixed and final, scholarship across the humanities and social sciences for decades now has shown us that identity is no such thing. Identity is not a fixed entity but rather an iterative process that is always open to change. We see this fact when dissenters refuse the erasure of Palestinian life and history and work to integrate Palestinian perspectives in Jewish narratives of self-understanding about Israel.

My dissertation shows that breaching the realm of tolerated dissent is not only a political offense, but also that dissenters locate and reveal the linchpin on which Zionist constructions of Jewish identity and history depends. The reinvention of identity appears so threatening because dissenters remove the linchpin and the Zionist rhetoric of justification collapses. From this collapse, solidarity activists reclaim Judaism from exclusionary ethnonationalism and reframe the threat of antisemitism as interconnected with—not uniquely separate from—other forms of racism, institutional violence, and dehumanization.

As I conclude this Epilogue, Nakba Day just occurred to commemorate seventy-three years since the mass expulsion in 1948, and Zionist settler colonialism and Israeli apartheid is playing out in broad daylight in Jerusalem with the violent dispossession of Palestinian residents from their neighborhood Sheikh Jarrah. Israeli crackdown on Palestinian protesters started escalating around Monday, May 10, 2021. Police violence and Israeli Jewish attacks targeting Palestinians have escalated throughout Jerusalem, including against worshippers at the Al Aqsa Mosque at the end of Ramadan. For the past eleven consecutive days and nights, Israel has once again bombed Gaza to destruction, Hamas has sent rocket fire, and 234 Palestinians and twelve Israeli Jews were killed, including more than sixty Palestinian children. The Israeli drone missiles and smart bombs destroying Gaza that are massacring Palestinian families, committing war crimes before our eyes, are funded by the United States. A ceasefire is supposed to start today, Friday, May 21, 2021.

Hundreds of thousands of people have been and continue to show at vigils and rallies around the world in support of the Palestinian people and their *sumud*, steadfast perseverance, to demand their unequivocal freedom. Together, we will end Israeli apartheid and build up a new world.

In Memoriam

Children killed by Israeli war crimes, May 2021[67]

We honor the memory of:

Rashid Mohammad Rashid Abu Arra, sixteen years old

Bashar Ahmad Ibrahim Samour, seventeen years old

Said Yousef Mohammad Odeh, sixteen years old

Rahaf Mohammad Attalla al-Masri, ten years old

and her cousin Yazan Sultan Mohammad al-Masri, two years old

brothers Marwan Yousef Attalla al-Masri, six years old

and Ibrahim Yousef Attalla al-Masri, eleven years old

Hussein Muneer Hussein Hamad, eleven years old

Ibrahim Abdullah Mohammad Hassanain, sixteen years old

Mohammed Saber Ibrahim Suleiman, fifteen years old

Mustafa Mohammad Mahmoud Obaid, sixteen years old

Baraa Wisam Ahmad al-Gharabli, five years old

Rahaf Mohammad Attalla Al-Masri, ten years old

Lina Iyad Fathi Sharir, fifteen years old

Zaid Mohammad Odeh Telbani, four years old

Hala Hussein Rafat Rifi, thirteen years old

Miriam Telbani, two years old, is missing and presumed dead

---

[67] This is an incomplete list, with as many names that I could find.

Hamza Mahmoud Yassin Ali, twelve years old

Hamada Attia Abed al-Emour, thirteen years old

Ammar Tayseer Mohammad el-Emour, ten years old

Elyan Moneer Ibrahim al-Emour, twelve years old

Yahya Mazen Shehada Khalifa, thirteen years old

Muhammad et-Tanani, three years old, and his three siblings, Ethem, four years old, Emir, five years old, and Ismail, six years old

Muhammed Zeyn el-Attar, five months old, and his siblings Islam, five years old, and Emire, six years old

Ibrahim ez-Zentisi, two years old

Zacharia Allus, seventeen years old

Rashid Ebu Ara, sixteen years old

Said Ude, sixteen years old

Zeyf Fadil Muhammed Kaysiye, seventeen years old

Obaida Jawabreh, seventeen years old

Eternal rest grant unto them, O God, and let perpetual light shine upon them. May the souls of the departed, through the mercy of God, rest in peace.

www.ingramcontent.com/pod-product-compliance
Lightning Source LLC
LaVergne TN
LVHW041317200726
843509LV00009B/529